It is a joy to com
Dovie to you. *A H*
from many years of fervent prayer, intense study, and personal experience. Mary's writings are certainly of a great spiritual nature, but they are also practical, relevant words for life today. Join Mary as she takes you to a "higher place." You will be glad you made the journey.

—Pastor Michael Green
Faith Church
New Orleans, Louisiana

I have known Mary Dovie for many years. Her love, zeal, and devotion to the Lord come through powerfully in this book. As you digest the pages of *A Higher Place in Him*, you will want to spend more time in His presence. In the secret place of the Most High is where we will be changed!

—Pastor David Newell
River of Life Church
Raleigh, North Carolina

Whether you have been a Christian for six months or sixty years, this book will bless you, so I encourage you to read *A Higher Place in Him* and allow the Lord to minister to you. This book reveals how deeply the Lord cherishes us, and it opens our heart even more to the generous and kind heart of the Father. This book can change your life if you apply the truths written in these pages, so I encourage you to draw closer to Him. It doesn't matter where you are in life, whether things are going well or going poorly; it isn't important whether you think you are living up to all the expectations of others or even those expectations you have imposed upon yourself. The only thing that matters is that He who is the lover of your soul is calling you to come to a higher place in Him.

—Apostle Willie F. Wooten
Gideon Christian Fellowship
New Orleans, Louisiana

A HIGHER PLACE IN HIM

MARY B. DOVIE

A STRANG COMPANY

A Higher Place in Him by Mary B. Dovie
Published by Creation House Press
A Strang Company
600 Rinehart Road
Lake Mary, Florida 32746
www.creationhouse.com

Cover design by Terry Clifton

Library of Congress Control Number: 2004101429

International Standard Book Number: 1–59185–555–1

04 05 06 07 08—987654321

Printed in the United States of America

To Abba, my Father
Jesus, my Lord
and
Holy Spirit, my Teacher and Inspirer
of this book

ACKNOWLEDGMENTS

The Lord does His work in such a way as to bring many people into a project just so He can bless them. Truly, I have been blessed by the people He has brought in to this publishing endeavor and privileged to experience the wonder of the Body of Christ. Here are the names of a few of God's children who have added value, encouragement, counsel, and direction to the publishing of this book.

I want to acknowledge the loving support of my entire family. My husband, Paul, has always believed and given me his full support. My sons, Matthew and Tony, have encouraged me and prayed for me.

My sister, Rosary Bullard, has been an inspiration, an editor, a prayer partner, and scriptural watchman. She has been a great influence on my life. I give thanks to the Lord for her and the entire Bullard clan from Plano, especially my niece, Jennifer Black, who is affectionately known as the "comma police."

Pastor Hank Sample has been my friend for more than eighteen years. He has been an editor, prayer partner, scriptural watchman, and teacher. The Lord is using him to train up a congregation that will not settle for anything less than spiritual intimacy with the Lord.

Apostle Willie Wooten has been an example of the high standard of personal commitment that the Lord is seeking from His children. He has been a scriptural watchman and counselor for this project.

Pastor David Newell, Pastor Mike Green, and Pastor Greg Tharel have been watchmen over this work, so as to maintain the spiritual integrity of the book.

The entire congregation of Joy Christian Church has stood as prayer warriors over the writing of this book. Their prayers continue to go up to the Throne Room on behalf of everyone who reads this book.

I want to thank Sister Jean Parsons for reading an early manuscript and giving me feedback about the significance of the Jewish wedding. My natural sister, Patricia Neyrey, and my sisters-in-Christ, Catherine Pollard, Irene Harron, and Jeanne Boudreaux, have encouraged me and prayed with me through the many years that it has taken for this book to be published. I thank the good people of Creation House Press and Strang Communications for catching the vision of this book and their hard work in bringing it to print.

> And whoever gives one of these little ones only a cup of cold water in the name of a disciple, assuredly, I say to you, he shall by no means lose his reward.
>
> —MATTHEW 10:42, NKJV

It is impossible to list every person individually who has been a blessing to me as this book was being birthed. I just know that each one will receive a reward from the Father, because I drank the spiritual cups of cold water they offered me when I was thirsty and weary.

Thank you, dear ones. May the Father's face always shine upon you. May you dance with the Lord at His wedding feast. May Holy Spirit lead you through the words of this book to a higher place in Him.

CONTENTS

FOREWORD

> Who may ascend into the hill of the Lord? And who may stand in His holy place? He who has clean hands and a pure heart, Who has not lifted up his soul to falsehood And has not sworn deceitfully. He shall receive a blessing from the Lord And righteousness from the God of his salvation. This is the generation of those who seek Him, Who seek Your face—even Jacob. Selah.
>
> —Psalm 24:3–6, nasb

A *Higher Place in Him* is about the all inclusiveness of God's wonderful salvation, His compassionate love, and most of all His great desire for an intimate loving relationship with His children. Mary Dovie, under the guidance and direction of the Holy Spirit, has done a remarkable job in capturing and sharing the heart of God.

For those of you who are hungry for the atmosphere and presence of God, this book is an invitation to meet Him in the Holy of Holies, where spiritual drought can no longer hinder you from achieving and accomplishing God's presence for your life in Christ Jesus. As Mary's pastor, I am honored to say that God has allowed her to paint, in words, using various colors to describe His ultimate plan for His church, individually and collectively.

To the church at large, page after page will excite your spirit and bring immense refreshment to your soul. I'm delighted to recommend to you an insightful reading adventure that if applied consistently and habitually, will change your life!

—Pastor Henry Sample
Joy Christian Church
New Orleans, Louisiana

PREFACE

In 1996 the Lord started to teach me about the High Places of Israel as I was reading through my One Year Bible. I began to study the scriptures in First and Second Kings that talked about the High Places and their significance. After looking up definitions and writing pages of notes, I knew that this information was important, but I did not know what the Lord wanted to do with it.

In August of 1999 our Church, Joy Christian Church, held a special ladies meeting, and I was asked to be the speaker. As I was preparing for this meeting, I felt a release as if the Lord was saying that it was time to use my notes about the High Places. Everyone who attended was blessed by the presence of the Lord. My husband, Paul, and Pastor Hank Sample attended the meeting. Paul encouraged me that night to write a book on the High Places. When I heard Paul say it, I knew immediately that I had always known it.

It is a strange thing how the Holy Spirit will drop such knowing and confidence into your spirit and mind suddenly. However, the Lord was not finished revealing the true heart of this book until May 2002. He had me rewrite the material to reflect His great compassionate love for mankind.

The main focus of the book changed from the High Places (a place of failure and loss) to the Lord's ultimate goal of drawing all men into *A Higher Place in Him*. This book has been commissioned by the Lord to present His great Plan of Love—Salvation—that is recorded in the Scriptures and the need of every man, woman, and child to willingly partake of its benefits.

The Lord is exposing the things that have hindered us from pressing into the greater benefits of the Covenant of the Cross in order to draw us closer to Him and keep us from stumbling and becoming prey for the evil one. Once the High Places of the heart are exposed we can begin to remove them through the work of the Spirit of God. This can only be achieved by pursuing an intimate relationship with the Lord, which is the desire of His heart.

I pray that as you read this material you will come to know the Lord in a more intimate way. It is my desire that you will continually walk in *A Higher Place in Him* everyday of your life.

INTRODUCTION

God wants to answer the cry of your heart. Even if you are not a Christian, He still wants to reveal His love to you and He wants to help you understand His great plan of salvation and how important it is to your life. If you already are a Christian, He wants to draw you into a deeper, more intimate relationship with Him and take you to *A Higher Place in Him*. He is working through every available method of communication to get this message to you and to anyone else who will listen.

This is nothing new; God has been communicating this same message for thousands of years as revealed in the Bible. His love and compassion for man is expressed in the Scriptures from Genesis through Revelation. The story of His love for man progressively unfolds throughout the Old Testament with the ultimate expression of His love revealed in the New Testament through the life of Jesus Christ. In every book He calls His covenant people to come to *A Higher Place in Him* so He can guide, protect, and reveal Himself to them.

The greatness of His love is demonstrated over and over again in the Old Testament especially during the times when

His covenant people turned away from Him and rejected His ways. God gave the Law to Moses to teach His people how they were to live and to ensure their safety from their enemies. Even as a good parent does today, He warned His people about what would cause them trouble and pain. He also taught them what would bring them prosperity and power. He went so far as to guarantee that if they would obey His words, He would supply these in abundance.

> Learn to do good; Seek justice, Rebuke the oppressor; Defend the fatherless, Plead for the widow. "Come now, and let us reason together," Says the LORD, "Though your sins are like scarlet, They shall be as white as snow; Though they are red like crimson, They shall be as wool. If you are willing and obedient, You shall eat the good of the land;
>
> —ISAIAH 1:17–19, NKJV

He sent judges and prophets to His people to raise their voices to call the people to walk according to His way when they went astray. The consummate symbols of Israel's wayward spiritual heart condition were the High Places of worship that were set up in the Promised Land in disobedience to the Law. (See 1 Kings 11:7;14:23.) The continued use and proliferation of the High Places by Israel were symbolic of their turning away from God. Although the High Places were geographic locations, they represented spiritual High Places that were within the hearts of the people. God contended for the heart of the people and sought to bring them into the place He prepared for them—*A Higher Place in Him*.

God includes the true record of His Old Covenant people in the Scriptures; their triumphs and failures as an example for future generations. (See 1 Cor. 10:1,6,11–12.) Their example is valid today and can help us avoid the hindrances that kept Israel from "eating the good of the land."

Throughout the New Testament, God continues to reveal His great love for man. The life, ministry, death, and resurrection of the Lord Jesus Christ revealed the lengths to which He is willing to go to express His love. The Sacrifice of the Cross is Jesus' proposal to every man, woman, and child that He is ready to commit Himself in a very real and intimate way. This proposal is initiated by Him and is offered to anyone who is willing to receive it as an invitation to intimate communion—*A Higher Place in Him*.

The Book of Acts and the Epistles provide guidance on how His New Covenant people, the Church, are to live. The Church has a great advantage over the Old Covenant people because of the work and ministry of the Holy Spirit. The Holy Spirit's job is to help, teach, guide, intercede for, and draw men to *A Higher Place in Him*. (See John 14:16–18; John 16:13.)

Even as in the Old Testament, God gives words of instruction and warning to His people in the New Testament. The messages to the seven churches of Asia are examples of how God continued to demonstrate His heart of love to man. These messages bring words of encouragement and warning about the spiritual heart conditions of each Church. The things that require rebuke are the same High Places of the heart that kept Israel from reaping the full riches of their covenant with God. Yet, He gives each Church a great promise to those who would overcome these hindrances and follow His instructions.

Three things that enable the believer to pursue a deeper relationship with the Lord are: *admit* that you need Him, *submit* to His Word in all areas of your life, and *commit* to follow Him no matter where He leads. "Let us know, Let us pursue the knowledge of the Lord. His going forth is established as the morning; He will come to us like the rain, Like the latter and former rain to the earth" (Hos. 6:3).

The Scriptures instruct us to turn to God because only through developing an intimate love relationship can we achieve the type of closeness He desires with us. He is calling us to rise above the High Places to walk in intimate fellowship with Him. He longs to keep us from stumbling over these hindrances and to take us to *A Higher Place in Him* where we can enjoy the fullness of our Covenant.

God is calling you to pursue an intimate relationship with Him. He has provided His Word to instruct you and the Holy Spirit to guide you every step of the way. His great love for you is unlimited and eternal. Every journey begins with the first step. He is inviting you through the words of this book to come and draw near to Him so you can experience *A Higher Place in Him*.

CHAPTER 1

GOD'S PLAN OF LOVE

> The Lord appeared to him from afar, saying, "I have loved you with an everlasting love; therefore I have drawn you with lovingkindness."
>
> —JEREMIAH 31:3, NAS

The Bible is the progressive revelation of God's love for man and His plan to restore mankind to a place of intimate fellowship with Him. In the Garden of Eden, Adam and Eve experienced intimate fellowship with God as disclosed in Genesis 3:8, "They heard the sound of the Lord God walking in the garden in the cool of the day." They knew the sound of God walking in the garden because this was the depth of fellowship they enjoyed with Him. God would come to the garden in the cool of the day and seek out Adam and Eve for companionship. He created them in His image and likeness and placed His glory on them.

> Then God said, "Let Us make man in Our image, according to Our likeness; and let them rule over the fish of the sea and over the birds of the sky and over the cattle and over all the earth, and over every

> creeping thing that creeps on the earth."
>
> —GENESIS 1:26, NAS

> What is man that You take thought of him, And the son of man that You care for him? Yet You have made him a little lower than God, And You crown him with glory and majesty!
>
> —PSALM 8:4–5, NASB

In the beginning, man was crowned with God's very own glory. Adam and Eve did not know they were naked, because they were clothed in the glory of God. This greatly puzzled the angels, as Psalm 8 revealed their questions and amazement. Man not only had a share of God's glory, but he was given free will—the God-given right to choose his own path. Man was created this way so he could be a real companion to God. Because he was given the freedom to choose, he could share the depths of God's heart through a mutual love relationship. The Lord described His love to Jeremiah by calling it an everlasting love. When God created man, He committed Himself to a love covenant that is eternal—forever.

When Adam and Eve's love commitment to God was tested, they failed the test. God was not caught by surprise. He already had a plan, since He is all-knowing and He knows the end of a thing at its beginning. (See Isa. 46:10.) God designed His plan to draw man back to Him through the progressive revelation of His everlasting love and mercy.

The plan and purpose of God that was set in motion in the Garden of Eden is still being carried out today. Even though civilizations have risen and fallen, the heart of God has not changed and His desire to restore man to his original status burns brightly. His plan of love involves every means of communication known to man. Second Timothy 3:16 explains the purpose of the written Word of God, "All Scripture is inspired by God and profitable for teaching, for reproof, for correction, for training in righteousness." Hebrews 1:1–4 explains the purpose of the life of Jesus Christ the incarnate Word of God, the Word of God made flesh.

> God, after He spoke long ago to the fathers in the prophets in many portions and in many ways, in these last days has spoken to us in His Son, whom He appointed heir of all things, through whom also He made the world. And He is the radiance of His glory and the exact representation of His nature, and upholds all things by the word of His power. When He had made purification of sins, He sat down at the right hand of the Majesty on high, having become as much better than the angels, as He has inherited a more excellent name than they.
>
> —HEBREWS 1:1–4, NAS

The good news or Gospel of Christ reveals that in Christ man is restored to his original status that was lost in the Garden of Eden. The love of God is expressed in its ultimate form through the life, ministry, death, and resurrection of Jesus Christ. Jesus has commissioned His followers to carry His message of deliverance and reconciliation to the world. (See Matt. 28:18–20.) This same message of God's plan of love is still being carried to the world today.

His love is everlasting and the depth of His love is exquisitely shown through the sacrifice of the Cross when He bore the sins of the world and reconciled man back to God. (See Isa. 53:10–11.) "And I, if I am lifted up from the earth, will draw all men to Myself," (John 12:32, NASB). The plan of love is to draw every man, woman, and child to God and restore each one of them to their original status, a companion of God, which is based on a mutual, freely given love.

Having a relationship with Him sounds so easy, especially when considering there is nothing too difficult for God. But, God has given man free will and has allowed him the right to choose whom he will love and follow. Free will makes it possible for man, through purposeful choice, to enter into a true love relationship, however it also gives man the opportunity and right to reject God's love.

God did this deliberately; He did not make a mistake. His plan of love is designed to make Himself vulnerable to you by unashamedly displaying His love for you even when you do not know Him or love Him. He knows that His love is strong enough to break through every hindrance in your life and draw you to a higher place in Him.

His heart yearns for your companionship and freely given love. He wants to teach you His ways of love so that you can be fully restored to Him. He wants to teach you about the things that hinder you from loving Him and enjoying His fellowship. He wants to stir up your desire to be restored to your original position, which was lost by Adam and Eve and reclaimed by Jesus. He calls out with His offer of everlasting love to anyone who will listen to come to a higher place in Him.

How will you respond?

CHAPTER 2

PREPARING THE WAY

> And I will make you a great nation, And I will bless you, And make your name great; And so you shall be a blessing; And I will bless those who bless you, And the one who curses you I will curse. And in you all the families of the earth will be blessed.
>
> —GENESIS 12:2–3, NASB

God's love plan required that a people, a nation, be set apart for the purpose of accomplishing His goal of restoring man to Himself. In the Book of Genesis the early history of mankind was recorded. Noah and his sons were chosen to be saved in the Ark because their bloodline was pure and untainted all the way back to Adam. (See Gen. 6:8–9.) The descendants of Noah repopulated the earth after the flood. From this people God chose Abraham to father a nation through which the Messiah, Jesus, would come.

The promise that God made to Abraham was passed down to his son, Isaac. Isaac had two sons, Esau and Jacob. The birthright and promise was passed down to Jacob and his descendants. God confirmed His covenant with Jacob and changed his name to Israel. On his deathbed Israel told Joseph that God would visit them in Egypt and bring them back into the land that was given to them by God. (See Gen. 15:13; 48:21.) Because He is ever true to His promises, at the appropriate time God commissioned Moses to take the nation of Israel out of Egypt and into the Promised Land.

> For you are a holy people to the LORD your God; the LORD your God has chosen you to be a people for His own possession out of all the peoples who are on the face of the earth. The LORD did not set His love on you nor choose you because you were more in number than any of the peoples, for you were the fewest of all peoples, but because the LORD loved you and kept the oath which He swore to your forefathers, the LORD brought you out by a mighty hand and redeemed you from the house of slavery, from the hand of Pharaoh king of Egypt. Know therefore that the LORD your God, He is God, the faithful God, who keeps His covenant and His lovingkindness to a thousandth generation with those who love Him and keep His commandments;
>
> —DEUTERONOMY 7:6–9, NAS

Israel became the Chosen People that God would use to accomplish the first part of His plan of love. Israel was to be a witness before all nations of God's love and willingness to covenant with mankind. They were given the Law, personally dictated by God to Moses, to teach them how to live. Their example was intended to show God's goodness and that His mercy is extended to all who love Him and keep His commandments.

> The Lord has today declared you to be His people, a treasured possession, as He promised you, and that you should keep all His commandments; and that He will set you high above all nations which He has made, for praise, fame, and honor; and that you shall be a consecrated people to the Lord your God, as He has spoken.
>
> —DEUTERONOMY 26:18–19, NASB

Jacob was set apart to participate in God's plan of love. God took a man and created a family. He took a family and created a nation. This nation was given a set of commandments called the Law of Moses that would teach them right from wrong and would prepare the hearts of men to recognize the Messiah—the ultimate expression of God's love. Israel was to be the keeper of the oracles of God, the Holy Scriptures. God commanded Moses to write down the laws of God to preserve the integrity of His Word from one generation to the next. Moses wrote the first five books of the Bible by the direct instruction of God.

Although Israel was the keeper of the Holy Scriptures, God did not restrict His message to Israel alone.

> But if a stranger sojourns with you, and celebrates the Passover to the Lord, let all his males be circumcised, and then let him come near to celebrate it; and he shall be like a native of the land. But no uncircumcised person may eat of it. The same Law shall apply to the native as to the stranger who sojourns among you.
>
> —Exodus 12:48–49, NASB

This inclusive statement showed Israel that God had commissioned them to bring the Law to the Gentile nations. If these nations followed God's commandments, He considered them to be equal with Israel under the Law.

Israel did not have an exclusive right to God's love. They were to carry the flame of God's burning love to a lost world. Through their obedience to the Law, they would prosper and the blessings of God would abound to their account. The nations of the world were to see the evidence of God's love in the greatness and prosperity of His Chosen People.

> Your word is a lamp to my feet and a light to my path.
>
> —Psalms 119:105, NASB

Israel stumbled and wavered in the commitment to follow the Word of God. Each generation had an obligation to prove themselves faithful to their calling. God was training up a nation. He sent prophets with words of kindness and love if they would return to Him. (See Isa. 1:17–19.) He told them what would happen if they continued to reject His Law. (See Deut. 28:15–68.) He ordered the prophets to write down His words as a witness so that when these things happened to them, Israel would understand why they occurred. Even though Israel abandoned God at times, God never abandoned Israel. He always extended hope to her if she would return to Him with her whole heart.

When you read the Old Testament accounts of God's dealings with Israel, look at the situation from God's point of view. God's plan of love is bigger than the history of one nation. Its paramount purpose is the restoration of mankind to a place of intimate fellowship with God. "The steps of a good man are ordered by the Lord, and He delights in his way. Though he fall, he shall not be utterly cast down; for the LORD upholds him with His hand," (Ps. 37:23–24, NKJV).

God's method of dealing with His backsliding nation reveals His boundless capacity for love and mercy. You can take comfort in the knowledge that His love for you is everlasting. If you stumble all you need to do is to call out to Him. He is ready to pick you up and teach you how to avoid repeating the same mistake and show you to a higher place in Him.

Don't hesitate to call on Him.

Chapter 3

THE ULTIMATE EXPRESSION OF LOVE

> For God so loved the world, that He gave His only begotten Son, that whoever believes in Him shall not perish, but have eternal life.
>
> —John 3:16, NASB

At the appointed time God sent His Son into the world as the ultimate expression of His love. The time of preparation was finished. The Word of God was made flesh and dwelt among mankind. The life of the Son, Jesus Christ, brought the full revelation of the Father's love. The Holy Scriptures, which Israel was given, proclaimed the Messiah, Jesus, as the coming Savior and King.

> But when the fullness of the time came, God sent forth His Son, born of a woman, born under the Law, so that He might redeem those who were under the Law, that we might receive the adoption as sons. Because you are sons, God has sent forth the Spirit of His Son into our

> hearts, crying, 'Abba! Father!' Therefore you are no longer a slave, but a son; and if a son, then an heir through God.
>
> —Galatians 4:4–7, NASB

The Law that Israel was given taught them right from wrong, but could not restore man to the original status he enjoyed in the Garden of Eden. God had to provide a legal way that would not merely cover sin like the Old Covenant sacrifices, but would remit sin and move it out of the way. This was the mission of the Messiah, Jesus. He would pay the price for Adam's love failure in the garden that had separated man from God.

> This is My commandment, that you love one another, just as I have loved you. Greater love has no one than this, that one lay down his life for his friends. You are My friends if you do what I command you. No longer do I call you slaves, for the slave does not know what his master is doing; but I have called you friends, for all things that I have heard from My Father I have made known to you.
>
> —John 15:12–15, NAS

Jesus stated the greatness of the Father's love over and over again. God the Father wanted to bring His children home, all the children of Adam, and there was nothing He would withhold to achieve His goal. His plan of love required the ultimate sacrifice to be the greatest expression of His love.

His sacrifice of love was even more astonishing when considered in the light of Israel's backsliding ways and her failure to be a credible witness of God's love to the other nations of the world. However, God faithfully kept His word to Israel and continued to reach out to her even when she rejected His Law. He sent His Son into the world to bring His message of love first to the Jew and then to the rest of the world. (See Rom. 1:16.)

> He was in the world, and the world was made through Him, and the world did not know Him. He came to His own, and those who were His own did not receive Him. But as many as received Him, to them He gave the right to become children of God, even to those who believe in His name, who were born, not of blood nor of the will of the flesh nor of the will of man, but of God.
>
> —JOHN 1:10–13, NAS

During the three and one-half years of His ministry, Jesus trained up His disciples to continue the work of God's plan of love after His ascension. "And He said to them, 'Go into all the world and preach the gospel to all creation,'" (Mark 16:15, NAS). Just as Israel had received the oracles of God and was commissioned to carry them to the world, so too were the followers of the Lord Jesus given a commission to bring the "good news" of reconciliation to the nations of the world.

> I will make your descendants as numerous as the stars in the sky and will give them all these lands, and through your offspring [seed] all nations on earth will be blessed.
>
> —GENESIS 26:4, NIV

> Therefore go and make disciples of all nations, baptizing them in the name of the Father and of the Son and of the Holy Spirit.
>
> —MATTHEW 28:19, NIV

God's family, the Church—the Body of Christ, is composed of people from all nations and is appointed to carry the message of His love. The Church now has the responsibility to be a witness to the world, just as Israel was called. However, the Church has a great advantage Israel did not have—He is the Holy Spirit. Because of the work of the Cross, the Holy Spirit indwells the followers of Christ when they receive Jesus as their Lord. He is sent to teach, guide, intercede for, and direct the work of the Body of Christ.

> But the Helper, the Holy Spirit, whom the Father will send in My name, He will teach you all things, and bring to your remembrance all that I said to you.
>
> —JOHN 14:26, NAS

The Holy Spirit's ministry and work continues today and will not be finished until God's plan of love achieves its purpose. Through His indwelling presence, the believer has the ability to commune with God even as Adam did in the garden in the cool of the day. This is a place of intimate fellowship and companionship that God desires to have with each of His children. It is a great privilege that every child of God has the ability to enjoy.

If you want to experience this type of fellowship with God, all you have to do is receive Jesus as Lord of your life. His offer of love is for anyone who is willing to receive it. He takes your sin and gives you His righteousness. Since the wages of sin is death, He pays off your debt with His death on the Cross and causes you to receive great spiritual blessings. (See Eph. 1:3;2:6.) If you have never asked Him into your heart, ask Him right now. If you have backslidden and turned away from Him, He is ready to receive you even as the prodigal was welcomed back by his father. If you have already given Him Lordship, then renew your vow to Him.

Pray this prayer with a sincere heart and cry out to Him so that you may receive what He is so willing to give you and begin your journey to a higher place in Him.

> *Father God,*
>
> *I come to you in Jesus' name. Your Word says that if I confess with my mouth the Lord Jesus, and shall believe in my heart that God has raised Him from the dead, I shall be saved. I choose to believe Your Word and I believe in the work of the Cross. I confess Jesus as my Lord. I believe in my heart that You raised Him from the dead and that He paid the price for my sins. Your Word says, "For with the*

heart a person believes, resulting in righteousness, and with the mouth he confesses, resulting in salvation." Based *on Your Word, I declare that I am the righteousness of God in Christ Jesus and that I am saved!*

Thank you, Father, in Jesus' name.

Welcome to the family of God!

CHAPTER 4

THE LORD'S PROPOSAL

Do not let your heart be troubled; believe in God, believe also in Me. In My Father's house are many dwelling places; if it were not so, I would have told you; for I go to prepare a place for you. If I go and prepare a place for you, I will come again and receive you to Myself, that where I am, there you may be also.

—JOHN 14:1–3, NASB

Jesus' words to His disciples on the night before His crucifixion were not merely words of comfort and promise. They were words used in the Jewish wedding contract and the disciples were well aware of their significance. The bridegroom would tell his betrothed, "I go and prepare a place for you," after she drank the cup of wine he offered her as a sign she accepted his marriage proposal. The "bride price" was not a set value, but would be negotiated between the bridegroom and the bride's father. The bridegroom would then pay the "bride price" to the girl's father and return home to his father to build a house. When the bridegroom's father was satisfied with the accommodations prepared by his son, he gave his son permission to go and retrieve his bride.[1]

Jesus paid the highest price for His bride, the Church, by offering His life on the Cross. Jesus was totally committed to doing the Father's will, yet when it came time to pay the "bride price" for His Church He had to wrestle with His human will of self-preservation.

> And He went a little beyond them, and fell on His face and prayed, saying, "My Father, if it is possible, let this cup pass from Me; yet not as I will, but as You will."
>
> —MATTHEW 26:39, NASB

The extreme price for His bride had been set by God the Father. Through His obedience to the Father's will, Jesus agreed to pay the price set by the Father, thereby valuing the souls of men to be worth His life.

The "bride price" must be paid for the marriage contract to be affirmed. Jesus paid the price and openly displayed His commitment to every man, woman, and child for all eternity by dying on the Cross. This was His responsibility as the bridegroom and He performed everything that was required of Him out of a heart of love and passion for His bride.

> Or do you not know that your body is a Temple of the Holy Spirit who is in you, whom you have from God, and that you are not your own? For you have been bought with a price: therefore glorify God in your body.
>
> —1 CORINTHIANS 6:19–20, NAS

[1]The reader is urged to do further study of the customs of a Jewish wedding. For an entertaining look at the specifics of a Jewish wedding, you can visit http://www.worshipradio.com/ZolaVideo.htm. Zola Levitt Ministries has a video called *Beloved Thief*, which is viewable online. For a more in-depth study, see Rabbi Aryeh Kaplan's book, *Made in Heaven: A Jewish Wedding Guide*, published by Moznaim Publishing Corporation, June 1983. The book is available on Amazon.com

The Church of the Lord Jesus Christ is the bride of Christ. Every member of the Church is betrothed to the Lord Jesus through the covenant of the Cross. As the believer works out his salvation through the renewing of his mind, he must take on the responsibility of the bride to prepare himself for the Lord's coming.

To bring clarity on the subject of the bride's responsibility, I have included an email from my sister, Patricia Neyrey.

Excerpt of an Email From My Sister, Patricia: October 5, 1999

I have come to understand what Jesus meant when He said to me at the retreat in Arkansas, "The trees and sky and water and mountains were gifts, but the Cross was My commitment to you. That's why I am no longer satisfied with gifts from you; I want a commitment."

I now understand He was proposing to me! In my works-oriented mind, I thought He wanted me to put out the trash more often. No, He was proposing to me. He wants to be my everything, my everyone! He wants to be the One I turn to for love, protection, understanding, salvation, teaching, deliverance, and everything else. He wants me to lean on Him, to look to Him, and to love spending time with Him. I looked up the scriptures in Zechariah about the filthy rags on Joshua (Zech. 3:4) and *I SAW IT!* I read it and *I SAW IT!*

This is a picture of Jesus and us. Jesus took our rags and gave us His robes of righteousness. I am not the same. The old person is dead and gone. Jesus picked me up out of the trash heap and washed me in His blood—dressed me in fine robes, put a ring on my finger, loved me, and made me new. But, when I confess, "I have a problem with pride, I have a hard time forgiving others,...blah...blah...blah," what I am doing is jumping back into the trash heap and

> wallowing in the mud again. I'm saying to Jesus, "What you did for me was really nothing! I'll just go wallow back in the mud, if you don't mind!"
>
> Now the big challenge is to recognize the tests and the siftings when they appear. Most of the time, the really big tests of our faith look so normal, so trite, and so unimportant. But, it is the little foxes that mess us up. We must always remember to wait and think before we respond. Usually, the knee-jerk reaction will be in the flesh. We are ready to take that leap right back into the mud puddle, because it is comfortable and the slope is so steep and so easy to slip back into. The mountain is harder to climb up, but that is where the Lord is!

The first step in fulfilling our responsibilities in this covenant is to realize that we have our part to contribute in this relationship. A true love relationship requires each party to invest their love, time, effort, and attention to nurture the fellowship if it is to deepen and grow in intimacy. The value Jesus put on His Church was His own life. "Greater love has no one than this, that one lay down his life for his friends" (John 15:13, NAS). It is now time for His Church to prepare herself for His glorious return.

Growing in intimacy does not just happen; it must progress over time and overcome the obstacles that arise. These hindrances arise from several sources, but the most dangerous ones are the normal, seemingly harmless challenges to faith that present themselves everyday. It is first necessary to recognize them as obstacles before they can be removed. Since the Bible is the progressive revelation of God's dealings with man, it is the best source for uncovering the hindrances, snares, and traps, the High Places of the heart, that thwart the development of our love relationship with the Lord.

The bridegroom, Jesus, has fulfilled His responsibility in the marriage contract by paying the established "bride price" for His Church. While the Church waits for His return, she must fulfill her responsibility in the marriage contract by preparing herself for His coming.

The believer is not in this alone, but has been given the Great Comforter to lead and guide him. The obstacles and hindrances, the High Places of the heart, can only be torn down through the work of the Holy Spirit in the committed child of God.

He is ready to answer the cry of your heart, if you are ready to let Him work through you and in you to take you to a higher place in Him.

CHAPTER 5

ISRAEL'S PART WAS OBEDIENCE

> Now these things happened to them [Israel] as an example, and they were written for our instruction, upon whom the ends of the ages have come. Therefore let him who thinks he stands take heed that he does not fall.
> —1 CORINTHIANS 10:11–12, NASB

God was faithful to His covenant with the people of Israel. He chose Abraham to be the father of a nation from which the Messiah, Jesus, would come. He brought them out of Egypt with His mighty power and sustained them in the desert with miracle after miracle. God showed Himself strong on their behalf. But, Israel had their part to contribute to this alliance. On several occasions God, through Moses, Joshua, Elijah, and many others, allowed Israel to choose whether to follow the Lord God or not. In Joshua 24:24 the people pledged their obedience to God. "The people said to Joshua, 'We will serve the Lord our God and we will obey His voice.'" Joshua commanded the people to set up markers as reminders and witnesses to the covenant they had made. These monuments were to be symbols for the people and future generations to remember their sworn allegiance to the Lord.

God chose Israel and He called them to be holy. The Lord gave Israel the Law to guide them how to live. "For I am the LORD your God. Consecrate yourselves therefore, and be holy, for I am holy," (Lev. 11:44, NAS). They were to imitate God by living according to the code of holiness, the Law of Moses. In Leviticus 23, the Lord gave Moses the order and manner of the Feasts of the Lord. Israel was charged to observe these feasts in the proper way and at the proper time.

> And the LORD spoke to Moses, saying, "Speak to the children of Israel, and say to them: The feasts of the LORD, which you shall proclaim to be holy convocations, these are My feasts."
>
> —LEVITICUS 23:1–2, NKJV

God established seven feasts that Israel was to keep every year. They were the feasts of Passover, Unleavened Bread, First Fruits, Weeks, Trumpets, Day of Atonement, and Tabernacles. Although Israel was unaware of it, each of these feasts caused them to rehearse over and over again signs that pointed to the Messiah, Jesus. God, in His mercy, gave Israel these feasts to observe as part of their participation in His plan of love.

Because the feasts and the order of the daily sacrifices all pointed to the Messiah, Jesus, God could not tolerate any changes in the way Israel observed them. The order and place of the sacrifices each had a connection to an eternal plan that was not known to Israel. The revelation of this plan was progressive over time. The feasts and the Law were given as guides for the people to follow so that God could train them up to be witnesses of His love to all nations.

In addition to the feasts and Law, God designed the tabernacle of Moses as a representation of His plan of love. (See

Exod. 25–31.) The Temple of God that was built later in Jerusalem was designed according to the tabernacle of Moses that was given to Israel in the desert along with the Law. (See 1 Kings 5–6.) The layout of the Temple was an illustrative representation of God's plan of love. As the priest progressed from the bronze altar, to the bronze laver for washing, into the outer room with the lampstand, showbread, and altar of incense, and then finally into the Holy of Holies, the very presence of God, he saw a visual display of God's plan of love and how it was to unfold. All of these things were done with an eternal purpose in mind. Israel's responsibility was to obey and observe the Lord's commandments.[2]

God commanded the men of Israel to present themselves three times a year before Him in the Temple. The Temple was the place where the presence of the Lord God dwelt among the people. God wanted them to come to the place of His presence to be with Him physically and to observe the physical representation of His plan of love as demonstrated in the Temple. As the men of Israel followed God's instruction, He was training them to recognize Jesus as the only way for mankind to be reconciled to God.

The sacrifices, the feasts, the Temple, and the Law were established as symbols that God used to train Israel about His plan of love. Israel's part was to obediently follow God's instructions and to learn from them about His great love. Even though they did not understand why God commanded them to do certain things, it was Israel's part to obey and to trust the Lord God. He had proven Himself faithful on their behalf when He brought them out of Egypt with a mighty hand. God proved Himself faithful throughout the journey in the wilderness with signs and wonders. He continued to be

[2]The reader is encouraged to study the tabernacle of Moses in greater depth. M. R. Dehaan, MD wrote a book on the subject entitled *The Tablernacle*, published by Zondervan Publishing House.

faithful when they went in to possess the Promised Land. Israel's responsibility was to prove herself by her obedience to the Lord's commands and to trust Him to perform His word.

> But My people did not listen to My voice, and Israel did not obey Me. So I gave them over to the stubbornness of their heart, to walk in their own devices. Oh that My people would listen to Me, that Israel would walk in My ways!
>
> —PSALM 81:11–13, NAS

Israel disobeyed God's instructions and withdrew from the One Who redeemed them from slavery and gave them their own land. But, even in their rebellion God called them to return to obedience and to walk according to His Law. Israel's failure did not ruin God's plan, but it limited them from enjoying the fullness of their covenant with Him.

God's dealings with Israel exhibited the wonders of His mercy. While Israel turned away from God, He still extended His hand, His love, and His forgiveness, if they would repent. Israel's example was recorded in the holy Scriptures as a warning to the people of God, both Old and New Covenant people.

Even as God patiently trained Israel through the progressive revelation of His love and by exposing her ways, He is still doing this today. Take advantage of this time to consider His great mercy and love that is extended to everyone who calls on His name and desires to walk in a higher place in Him.

He desires to hear from you and is ready to respond to your call.

CHAPTER 6

HIGH PLACES: A SYMBOL OF REBELLION

> Then you shall drive out all the inhabitants of the land from before you, and destroy all their figured stones, and destroy all their molten images and demolish all their high places; and you shall take possession of the land and live in it, for I have given the land to you to possess it.
>
> —NUMBERS 33:52–53, NAS

Israel was commissioned by God to possess the Promised Land. They were commanded to destroy the vestiges of idolatrous worship that the previous inhabitants had established throughout the land. These places of worship were in the hills and mountains, so they became known as the High Places. God required Israel to purge the land in this manner to keep them from being seduced into following after other gods. "But if you do not drive out the inhabitants of the land from before you, then it shall come about that those whom you let remain of them will become as pricks in your eyes and as thorns in your sides, and they will trouble you in the land in which you live," (Num. 33:55, NASB).

> Do you thus repay the LORD, O foolish and unwise people? Is not He your Father who has bought you? He has made you and established you.
>
> —DEUTERONOMY 32:6, NAS

As a good parent, God warned the children of Israel about the dangers in the Promised Land. There were not just physical dangers, but spiritual snares and traps that needed to be dealt with in order for them to live in the fullness of their covenant with Him. The High Places represented the waywardness of following after other gods that would eventually cause the children of Israel to go into captivity. God was training Israel to follow His voice so they could prosper and enjoy their place as His Chosen People.

> Train up a child in the way he should go, even when he is old he will not depart from it.
>
> —PROVERBS 22:6, NAS

God was not just training up one child, but He was rearing a nation of people over thousands of years and countless generations. He established rules for living that would serve and direct Israel throughout the ages. Then He instituted the New Covenant, which was far better than the first.

> Do we not all have one father? Has not one God created us? Why do we deal treacherously each against his brother so as to profane the covenant of our fathers?
>
> —MALACHI 2:10, NAS

God sent prophets to carry His message of rebuke and to call His people back to the right way of living. At times His words seemed harsh and extremely stern, but there was so much at stake that only the unvarnished truth had the power to break the cycle of Israel's backsliding. God established the standard for parenting through the practice of tough love in which the parent requires the child to take responsibility for his actions and bear the consequences. Even as good parents suffer along with their children through these times, God suffered along with Israel through her times of rebellion.

> And they said to him [Samuel], "Behold, you have grown old, and your sons do not walk in your ways. Now appoint a king for us to judge us like all the nations." But the thing was displeasing in the sight of Samuel when they said, "Give us a king to judge us."And Samuel prayed to the LORD. The LORD said to Samuel, "Listen to the voice of the people in regard to all that they say to you, for they have not rejected you, but they have rejected Me from being king over them."
>
> —1 SAMUEL 8:5–7, NASB

Israel's desire to be like other nations, effectively was a rejection of God as their King. They had been warned to purge the land to avoid the physical and spiritual snares that were there. By allowing idol-worshiping among them, the Israelites became corrupted. (See 1 Cor. 15:33.) Israel was supposed to be the example for the other nations to follow. Instead they became snared by the culture and traditions of their neighbors.

Israel adopted the High Places of worship that other nations had set up and continued to use to worship their gods. They started by worshiping the Lord God at these places, this way they could fit in with the other nations and still worship the God of Israel. They compromised the Law of God with their added embellishments and exalted their own ways in the eyes of God. However, eventually they fell into even worse transgressions, for if it was good to worship the Lord at the High Places, perhaps it might also be good to worship Baal, Molech, Ashterah, and other assorted "deities" there as well. Mixing the worship of false gods with the worship of the Lord God implied that there were many ways of salvation and hope. God could not accept these embellishments because His great plan of love was too important. There were eternal reasons why Israel was commanded to worship a specific way. There was only one way, God's way. Only one place had been established by God where His people's sacrifices would be accepted and His Presence would reside.

The continued use and proliferation of the High Places by Israel were symbolic of their rebellion against the Law of God. Although the High Places were geographic locations, they represented spiritual High Places that were within the hearts of the people. Before the physical High Places could be destroyed, never to be rebuilt, the High Places in the hearts of the people had to be torn down.

> And Samuel said, "Has the LORD as much delight in burnt offerings and sacrifices as in obeying the voice of the LORD? Behold, to obey is better than sacrifice, and to heed than the fat of rams."
>
> —1 SAMUEL 15:22, NAS

From God's point of view obedience is better than rituals and ceremonies. Rituals and ceremonies do not require relationship, but true obedience does. A good child obeys his parents' instructions because he loves them and does not want to hurt or displease them. This is what God is looking for today and what He wanted from Israel. He wants your obedience to be rooted and grounded in your sincere love for Him. He is the Great Lover of your soul and wants you to reciprocate with a commitment of love to Him through obedience to His Word.

> He who has My commandments and keeps them is the one who loves Me; and he who loves Me will be loved by My Father, and I will love him and will disclose Myself to him.
>
> —JOHN 14:21, NASB

Receive His sweet words of love as He speaks into your life as you walk along the path to a higher place in Him.

CHAPTER 7

HIGH PLACES: THE KINGS' INFLUENCE

...Give us a king to judge us.

—1 SAMUEL 8:6, NAS

The people of Israel went to the prophet Samuel and demanded that he appoint a king to judge them like all the other nations. (See 1 Sam. 8:5–8.) Samuel was upset about this request and went to seek counsel from God about it. God revealed to Samuel that the people were not rejecting him as prophet, but they were rejecting God as their King. God gave the people what they asked for, but sent Samuel to testify in their hearing what their kings would do. (See 1 Sam. 8:10–20.)

God knew that Israel would cry out for a king. He gave Moses the instructions for how a king should live and what he needed to do to keep from straying from God's ways. These instructions were written in the Book of Deuteronomy 17:14–20. The king was instructed to write a copy of the Law in his own writing under the guidance of the priests. The king was told to keep this copy for his personal devotional reading. This was God's way of training up the king to keep the Law so that the people would be blessed through the king's obedience to God's plan of love.

> It shall be with him [the king] and he shall read it all the days of his life, that he may learn to fear the LORD his God, by carefully observing all the words of this Law and these statutes, that his heart may not be lifted up above his countrymen and that he may not turn aside from the commandment, to the right or the left, so that he and his sons may continue long in his kingdom in the midst of Israel.
>
> —DEUTERONOMY 17:19–20, NASB

The kings of Israel wielded power over the people not only to demand taxes and servitude of the people, but as an influence for either the cause of good or evil. Solomon was lauded as a great and wise king of Israel who had favor with God and man. He followed through on his father's, King David's, plan to build the Temple of the Lord God in Jerusalem. God blessed Solomon with great wisdom because of his obedience to God's Word in the early years of his life. Solomon stayed the course until, in his old age, he allowed himself to compromise the commands of God for the desires of his heathen wives. (See 1 Kings 11:1–13.)

> Solomon did what was evil in the sight of the LORD, and did not follow the LORD fully, as David his father had done. Then Solomon built a high place for Chemosh the detestable idol of Moab, on the mountain which is east of Jerusalem, and for Molech the detestable idol of the sons of Ammon. Thus also he did for all his foreign wives, who burned incense and sacrificed to their gods.
>
> —1 KINGS 11:6–8, NASB

Instead of holding fast to the Law of Moses, Solomon turned from solely following the Lord God and set an example for Israel that brought destruction. His sin culminated in the dispersion of the people of Israel among the nations. Solomon took heathen wives, which was strictly forbidden by the Law of Moses. (See Deut. 17:14–20.) Consequently, in his old age he built high places for his heathen wives to worship their gods. By establishing the high places for his wives, Solomon's actions condoned the heathen practices that the Law of Moses had forbidden. Solomon, who was once the greatest of the kings of the earth, became the king responsible for the division of the kingdom and enmity between the tribes.

In the books of First and Second Kings God repeatedly admonished the kings for failing to tear down the high places in the land. Even the kings God recognized for their good deeds did not tear down the high places of worship that had been established under the rule of the previous kings. By this time high place worship had degenerated to the point that the people were worshiping idols like Solomon's heathen wives.

> He [Jehoshaphat] walked in all the way of Asa his father; he did not turn aside from it, doing right in the sight of the LORD. However, the high places were not taken away; the people still sacrificed and burnt incense on the high places.
>
> —1 KINGS 22:43, NAS

With each passing generation, the people of Israel turned farther away from the true ways of God. The story of these kings was one of constant missed opportunity. God sent prophets to warn the king and the people to return to living according to the commands of the Lord.

> Go and proclaim these words toward the north and say, "return, faithless Israel,"declares the LORD; "I will not look upon you in anger. For I am gracious," declares the LORD; "I will not be angry forever. Only acknowledge your iniquity, that you have transgressed against the LORD your God and have scattered your

> favors to the strangers under every green tree, and you have not obeyed My voice," declares the Lord.
>
> —Jeremiah 3:12–13, nas

But the people and their kings would not submit themselves to the Law of God. There were two kings who did tear down the High Places. However, by the time of these kings, the High Place worship was so ingrained in their cultural traditions, the people eagerly rebuilt the High Places as soon as the next king sat on the throne. Their cultural traditions had become more real to them than the Word of God.

> And My people who are called by My name humble themselves and pray and seek My face and turn from their wicked ways, then I will hear from heaven, will forgive their sin and will heal their land. Now My eyes will be open and My ears attentive to the prayer offered in this place [the Temple].
>
> —2 Chronicles 7:14–15, nasb

God's promise to Israel to receive them back into His good graces was always available to them. However, God limited the promise to prayers of repentance offered in the Temple, the place where His presence dwelt among the people. Prayers offered at the High Places were not acceptable in God's eyes. His great plan of love was visually displayed in the Temple and that was the place of acceptable prayer. However, their problem was not really their physical location, but the spiritual state of their hearts, which they had hardened to the Word of God and His great plan of love.

This spiritual heart condition derives from setting up High Places of the Heart. They are established when you place your will and desires above or equal to the will of God in your life. The result is the mixing of the worship of God and obedience to Him with the worship of the idols of your own making.

Everyday offers an opportunity to compromise with the cultural and societal norms of the day. But, God's love and mercy are relentlessly pursuing you through His great plan of love to take you to a higher place in Him. Spend time with Him and He will reveal Himself to you.

CHAPTER 8

GOD CALLED ISRAEL TO RETURN TO HIM

> Listen, O heavens, and hear, O earth; for the LORD speaks, "Sons I have reared and brought up, but they have revolted against Me....Wash yourselves, make yourselves clean; remove the evil of your deeds from My sight. Cease to do evil, learn to do good; seek justice, reprove the ruthless, defend the orphan, plead for the widow."
>
> —ISAIAH 1:2, 16–17, NAS

God used Isaiah to speak His heart to the rebellious children of Israel. Even in all their backsliding, God still called them His sons; the ones He trained up even as a natural father rears his children. Their treachery was not aimed at an aloof and distant god, but the Great One who separated them to be the Chosen People of God through whom He would manifest the ultimate expression of His love—the Messiah, Jesus.

God admonished the people of Israel to clean themselves

and to learn to do what is good. He had given them the Law to teach them how to live. Even the king was given specific instructions so that he would learn to do good, seek justice, reprove the wicked, and follow the rest of God's commands. God was committed to Israel even though they failed to live right and they worshiped other gods at the High Places. His great heart of love would not let Him disown Israel. As a good Father, He dealt with His disobedient children and as Husband contended for their love.

> Return, faithless people, declares the LORD, for I am your husband.
>
> —JEREMIAH 3:14, NIV

> How can I give you up, O Ephraim? How can I surrender you, O Israel? How can I make you like Admah? How can I treat you like Zeboiim? My heart is turned over within Me, all My compassions are kindled.
>
> —HOSEA 11:8, NAS

The struggle was for the heart of the people because God had given man the right to freely choose whom he would follow. When Israel pulled away from God, they fled from their protector and followed after evil. Instead of displaying before the nations of the world the prosperity of the blessed of the Lord God, they became an example of what happens to the nation who rebels against the commands of God. But, God's great plan of love would not be thwarted by Israel's failure; His love was greater than their faults. In fact, the magnitude of God's love was revealed in even greater power because He worked through a people who continually wavered in their commitment to Him.

> For the LORD will vindicate His people, and will have compassion on His servants, when He sees that their strength is gone, and there is none remaining, bond or free.
>
> —DEUTERONOMY 32:36, NASB

King Ahab and Jezebel, his wife, did despicable evil in the Northern Kingdom and turned the hearts of the people to do greater evil than any other king before him. Yet, when Ahab humbled himself before God by wearing sackcloth and ashes, God honored him and showed him mercy. "Do you see how Ahab has humbled himself before Me? Because he has humbled himself before Me, I will not bring the evil in his days, but I will bring the evil upon his house in his son's days," (1 Kings 21:29).

> Let the wicked forsake his way and the unrighteous man his thoughts; and let him return to the LORD, and He will have compassion on him, and to our God, for He will abundantly pardon.
>
> —ISAIAH 55:7, NASB

The example of God's mercy extended to King Ahab proved God to be faithful to keep His word even to the wicked Ahab. God's compassion and love were challenged by Israel's behavior as recorded in the Scriptures. Through His faithfulness to honor His commitment of love to His Chosen People, God established a witness and testimony to the greatness of His heart of love for all eternity. The story of Israel as told in the Scriptures was not sugarcoated to make God's Chosen People look good. It was told truthfully in order to relate the story of God's great plan of love. The triumphs and missed opportunities of His Old Covenant people were recorded as examples that exposed the depth of God's great love for man.

His love has not changed; He is still calling out to a lost and hurting world to come to Him. He wants to teach us how to live and to prosper as children of God. Society has changed and we have made great technological progress, but the heart of man is still the same. There is still that place in our hearts that only He can fill. By studying Israel's example, we can look into the spiritual heart condition that hindered them from enjoying the fullness of their covenant with God. These hindrances or High Places of the heart can have the same effect on our relationship with God if we allow them to be raised up in our lives.

The High Places of the heart are built up by the elevation of the will or man-made doctrines to the place of equality with or even above the Word of God. These High Places rest on the foundation of a self-sufficient attitude, an unwillingness to change, and the tendency to follow after anything that delights the senses; a spirit of fickleness. These hindrances do not suddenly appear in our lives; we are born with them as part of our sin nature. As such, we often are not even aware that they exist. If they are not dealt with they continue to develop. They hinder our relationship with the Lord like weeds encroaching on a garden. It is much easier to deal with weeds when we are vigilant and are watching for them than it is to wait until they have spread throughout the garden. In order to keep these weeds from growing back, it is necessary not only to deal with the symptoms, but also to attack the root, or foundation, of the problem to have total victory.

He will open the eyes of your understanding on the issues that are important to you. He will help you as you press in to achieve a higher place in Him.

Chapter 9

SELF-SUFFICIENT ATTITUDE: A HIGH PLACE

> When you [Israel] have eaten and are satisfied, you shall bless the Lord your God for the good land which He has given you. Beware that you do not forget the Lord your God by not keeping His commandments and His ordinances and His statutes which I am commanding you today;...Otherwise, you may say in your heart, "My power and the strength of my hand made me this wealth."
>
> —Deuteronomy 8:10–11,17, NASB

Israel was warned by God through the written Law to guard their hearts from forgetting the source of their blessings. God established Israel in the Promised Land and poured out His blessings in great abundance. But, there was a danger that in the midst of all this prosperity that Israel would begin to think that their own power and strength had brought the wealth. A self-sufficient attitude could only lead to destruction if it was allowed to take root in their hearts.

During the good times of plenty, Israel did allow a self-sufficient attitude to fill them with pride. They began to believe that their prosperity came to them because of an innate greatness, but their greatness actually stemmed from their association, or covenant, with the Lord God.

> Do not trust in princes, in mortal man, in whom there is no salvation.
>
> —PSALM 146:3, NAS

When troubles came to Israel, they were to turn to God first before seeking out alliances with other nations. King Asa of Judah, in the early part of his reign, sought the Lord and depended on Him in times of trouble. Asa prospered because the Lord's hand was upon him. However, in his latter days when Baasha, King of Israel (Samaria), came against the land, Asa turned to the Syrians for help. Asa did not seek the Lord because during the times of peace and prosperity his heart became lifted up in pride and self-sufficiency. God sent the seer Hanani to rebuke Asa.

> And at that time Hanani the seer came to Asa king of Judah, and said to him: "Because you have relied on the king of Syria, and have not relied on the LORD your God, therefore the army of the king of Syria has escaped from your hand. Were the Ethiopians and the Lubim not a huge army with very many chariots and horsemen? Yet, because you relied on the LORD, He delivered them into your hand."
>
> —2 CHRONICLES 16:7–8, NKJV

Asa responded to the Lord's rebuke in anger and put Hanani in prison and brutally oppressed some of the people. (See 2 Chron. 16:10.) Three years later, Asa became diseased in his feet. Although his disease was severe, he would not admit his sin and seek the Lord for healing. He died within two years. Like Solomon, Asa started out walking with the Lord, but later his heart was lifted up in pride because of the magnitude of the blessings and prosperity Israel experienced. He forgot that all of this wealth came from God and was the result of Israel's obedience and dependence on God.

"Thus says the LORD, 'Cursed is the man who trusts in mankind and makes flesh his strength, and whose heart turns away from the LORD,'" (Jer. 17:5, NAS). Asa reaped a curse from his act of anger and rebellion against the rebuke of the Lord. During the two years of his progressively worsening illness, Asa refused to make amends with God, so he died a sick and bitter man.

This cycle of starting out depending on the Lord God during times of war and national peril, then growing prideful with an attitude of self-sufficiency was repeated over and over throughout the history of God's Chosen People. God used many examples to show Israel that their victories were not because of their natural greatness, but because of His delivering mercy and love. In the days of Gideon, God delivered a victory to Israel with an army of three hundred against an invading army of tens of thousands of men. (See Judg. 7.) In the days of King Jehoshaphat of Judah, when three armies encamped against them to make war, God told Judah to march into battle with the singers and musicians leading the way singing praises to God. The spoils from this great victory were so plentiful that it took Judah three days to collect it. (See 2 Chron. 20.)

> He who trusts in his own heart is a fool, but he who walks wisely will be delivered.
>
> —PROVERBS 28:26, NAS

When God's Chosen People admitted they needed God and depended upon Him in times of trouble, He always delivered them. Even when in the natural world there seemed to be no way possible for Israel to be victorious, God would step in and spectacular things happened that only God could do. The key to their success was in humbling themselves before God and admitting they needed Him. By recognizing their dependence on God, they acknowledged that they could not save themselves.

A major theme in God's plan of love is for man to realize that he is a sinner and cannot save himself. Only a sinless man could pay the price of sin for the sinner by offering himself as a substitute for the transgressor. One of the major foundations of your love relationship with the Lord is admitting that you need Him.

> I [Jesus] am the vine, you are the branches. He who abides in Me, and I in him, bears much fruit; for without Me you can do nothing.
>
> —JOHN 15:5, NKJV

Today we have a sophisticated society that fosters a self-sufficient attitude. Among the snares and traps of our age are advanced technology, the exaltation of natural knowledge, and great material wealth. James 1:17 reminds us, "Every good gift and every perfect gift is from above, and comes down from the Father of lights, with whom there is no variation or shadow of turning," (NKJV). The source of all blessings is our loving Father. Every witty invention comes from the mind of God by His permission and consent. (See Prov. 8:12.)

The current world system promotes an "I'll do it my way" mind-set. It is very easy to operate this way in our daily lives because that is what is natural to our human, fallen, nature. However, God wants to lift us higher. Admitting that we need Him is a major step in our relationship with Him. When we sincerely admit our dependence on the Lord, we open the door of our hearts to Him.

> Behold, I stand at the door and knock; if anyone hears My voice and opens the door, I will come in to him, and will dine with him, and he with Me.
>
> —REVELATION 3:20, NAS

Tell Him that you need Him. Ask Him to come in and fellowship. He is waiting to reveal to you a higher place in Him.

CHAPTER 10

UNWILLINGNESS TO CHANGE: A HIGH PLACE

> They have turned their back to Me and not their face; though I taught them, teaching again and again, they would not listen and receive instruction.
>
> —JEREMIAH 32:33, NASB

Through the prophet Jeremiah, the Lord God lamented the spiritual heart condition of His covenant people. Their hearts had become unteachable, stubborn, intransigent, and self-willed. God had given them the Law to teach them how to live and prosper under their covenant with Him, yet they willfully refused to follow it, choosing their own way instead. Unwillingness on the part of the Israelites to change their ways eventually resulted in captivity for the nation.

> He [Jehoshaphat] walked in the way of his father Asa and did not depart from it, doing right in the sight of the LORD. The high places, however, were not

> removed; the people had not yet directed their hearts to the God of their fathers.
>
> —2 Chronicles 20:32–33, NASB

The people had elevated their will and their man-made doctrines (traditions) above the Word of God at the High Places. Their actions declared that they would worship God their own way—no matter what God said about it in His Word. The High Places were a prime example of their self-will in action. The incense burnings and heathen rituals that started on the High Places later migrated into the cities—on every housetop, on every corner, and even in the Most Holy Temple of the Lord God.

> Son of man, you live in the midst of the rebellious house, who have eyes to see but do not see, ears to hear but do not hear; for they are a rebellious house.
>
> —Ezekiel 12:2, NAS

God continued to reach out to His people even while they were in captivity to teach them and train them up, as a good father would do with his children. God told Ezekiel that the children of Israel had the ability to change their ways, but their rebellious and unteachable hearts refused to do it. They were using their legal right of free will to reject the Law of God. They not only turned their back on the Person of the Lord God, but also on His great plan of love to redeem mankind.

> So Samuel said: "Has the Lord as great delight in burnt offerings and sacrifices, as in obeying the voice of the Lord? Behold, to obey is better than sacrifice, and to heed than the fat of rams. For rebellion is as the sin of witchcraft, and stubbornness is as iniquity and idolatry. Because you have rejected the word of the Lord, He also has rejected you [Saul] from being king."
>
> —1 Samuel 15:22–23, NKJV

The prophet Samuel had long before declared God's opinion of rebellion and stubbornness. God had warned that from His point of view, rebellion was equivalent to witchcraft and stubbornness was the same as idol worship. Both Saul and the people had failed their test of obedience. Saul's excuse was that "the people made me do it." The Lord had made Saul king of Israel and what the king said was Law. Saul had the responsibility to hold fast to the commands of the Lord and see to it that they were followed. Saul and the army had decided that instead of destroying all the livestock as God commanded, they should save the best of them and make a grand display of offering them in a religious service to the Lord on an altar. The *form* of worship was becoming more important than *whom* they were worshiping and *how* He wanted to be worshiped. This revelation the Lord sent Samuel to deliver to Saul and the people went unheeded, not only by them, but also by the following generations.

> The king [Josiah] stood by the pillar and made a covenant before the LORD, to walk after the LORD, and to keep His commandments and His testimonies and His statutes with all his heart and all his soul, to carry out the words of this covenant that were written in this book. And all the people entered into the covenant.
>
> —2 KINGS 23:3, NASB

When the copy of the Law was discovered in the Temple, King Josiah of Judah rededicated the people to the Lord God. Because of the rebellion and stubbornness of the past kings and past generations, the Law of God had been lost to Josiah's generation. But, God's plan of love continued to work even through the dark days of rebellion and stubbornness of His Chosen People. Josiah responded to the Word of God with humility and submission, which was the only remedy for their spiritual heart condition.

> Not by way of eyeservice, as men-pleasers, but as slaves of Christ, doing the will of God from the heart.
>
> —Ephesians 6:6, NAS

> Submit therefore to God. Resist the devil and he will flee from you.
>
> —James 4:7, NAS

Submission to God's authority in your life is essential to enjoying the fullness of your covenant with Him. Following God's instructions for living is more important than doing things to please men or thinking up things to do to please God. God wants you to submit to His authority because you love Him not because you fear Him. Trust Him, because you realize that He knows your purpose better than you do. Only when you are fully submitted to Him can He use you and work through you.

> We have come to know and have believed the love which God has for us. God is love, and the one who abides in love abides in God, and God abides in him.
>
> —1 John 4:16, NASB

There is a tremendous difference between submission and agreement. God requires submission to His word and His way of living; He is not seeking agreement or approval. Agreement implies coming to a consensus, accord, or compromise between two parties. God's plan of love is rooted in the eternal and it is impossible for time-bound humans to fully comprehend its scope with their intellect. But, through a love relationship, you can trust Him because He has shown you the depth of His love through the work of the Cross. You can submit to His Word because that is how you show your love for Him.

> He who has My commandments and keeps them is the one who loves Me; and he who loves Me will be loved

> by My Father, and I will love him and will disclose Myself to him.
>
> —JOHN 14:21, NAS

Let His Word have preeminence in your life. Submit to His Lordship and He will reveal Himself to you and you will progress to a higher place in Him.

Chapter 11

FICKLENESS: A HIGH PLACE

> Beware that you are not ensnared to follow them, after they are destroyed before you, and that you do not inquire after their gods, saying, "How do these nations serve their gods, that I also may do likewise?"
>
> —Deuteronomy 12:30, NAS

Israel's fickle heart led her to follow after anything that delighted the senses. She disregarded the commission for which she was chosen by vacillating in her observance of the Law. Israel was to be the example to the nations as she walked in her covenant with the Lord God. He promised to exalt her above all nations if she followed after His commands. (See Deut. 28:1–14.) Israel was to set the standard that demonstrated the greatness of the Lord God's love for man. The other nations would see their witness and want to be like Israel so they could be blessed too.

Instead of staying committed to their covenant with the Lord God, they sought to be like the other nations. (See 1 Sam. 8:20.) With each generation their inconsistent regard for the Law led them to look to the heathen nations as their example. When King Ahaz of Judah visited King Tiglath-Pileser of Assyria, he saw a great altar in Damascus dedicated to a heathen god. He copied the pattern and had Urijah, the priest, build one like it in the Temple at Jerusalem. Then Ahaz used this heathen-designed altar, instead of the bronze altar that was designed by the Lord God, for the Temple's burnt offerings. (See Exod. 38:1–7; 2 Kings 16:10–15.)

> They rejected His statutes and His covenant which He made with their fathers and His warnings with which He warned them. And they followed vanity and became vain, and went after the nations which surrounded them, concerning which the LORD had commanded them not to do like them.
>
> —2 KINGS 17:15, NASB

Although God's Chosen People wavered in their commitment to God, God did not waver in His commitment to them. Even as a good parent warns his children about not following the gang and not to do something just because "everyone is doing it," God continued to reach out to His covenant people. He knew that Israel did not understand the important role she was to play in His great plan of love. She wanted to be like other nations, but she could not because God had called her to greatness. She was the Chosen People through whom the Messiah, Jesus, would come and redeem the world.

> He [Hezekiah] did right in the sight of the LORD, according to all that his father David had done. He removed the high places and broke down the sacred pillars and cut down the Asherah. He also broke in pieces the bronze serpent that Moses had made, for until those days the sons of Israel burned incense to it; and it was called Nehushtan. He trusted in the LORD, the God of Israel; so that after him there was none like him among all the kings of Judah, nor among those who were before him. For he clung to the LORD; he did

> not depart from following Him, but kept His commandments, which the LORD had commanded Moses.
>
> —2 KINGS 18:3–6, NASB

Hezekiah followed his father Ahaz on the throne. He turned away from following other nations and committed himself to follow God's commandments written in the Law. Hezekiah tore down the High Places and destroyed the idols that had been erected in the land of Judah. He elevated the commandments of God above the traditions of his society with its blend of heathen culture. His enemies took Hezekiah to task because he tore down the High Places. Rabshakeh from Assyria stood by the aqueduct outside the city of Jerusalem and called out to the people in the Hebrew language. He accused Hezekiah of taking down the High Places, thereby angering the Lord God. (See 2 Kings 18:22.) Rabshakeh did this to incite the people against Hezekiah because he knew that many of the people disagreed with this action. God delivered Hezekiah and Jerusalem because he sought the Lord and prayed. God sent Isaiah with a prophetic word and sent an angel into the enemy's camp that killed 185,000 Assyrians in one night. (See 2 Kings 19:20–37.)

Again God demonstrated His willingness to forgive and deliver His people when they returned to following Him. The tenderness of His heart and faithful commitment to His people continued to be revealed every time they repented. Hezekiah realized that the nation had to commit to God not just with words, but also with deeds. The High Places were visual symbols of their fickle hearts and had to be torn down to expose the depth of his commitment to God. Such a demonstration of loyalty deserved a spectacular response from the Lord God, so God simply wiped out an entire army over night.

> Do not love the world nor the things in the world. If anyone loves the world, the love of the Father is not in him. For all that is in the world, the lust of the flesh and the lust of the eyes and the boastful pride of life, is not

> from the Father, but is from the world. The world is passing away, and also its lusts; but the one who does the will of God lives forever.
>
> —1 JOHN 2:15–17, NASB

God has called us to commit ourselves to Him. Through the Cross His commitment to the world was unashamedly displayed for the entire world to see. He has called everyone who receives Him a child of God. He has given each one of us an inheritance as members of the family of God and the right to be called by His name.

> For as many as are led by the Spirit of God, these are sons of God. For you did not receive the spirit of bondage again to fear, but you received the Spirit of adoption by whom we cry out, "Abba, Father." The Spirit Himself bears witness with our spirit that we are children of God, and if children, then heirs—heirs of God and joint heirs with Christ, if indeed we suffer with Him, that we may also be glorified together.
>
> —ROMANS 8:14–17, NKJV

Being led by the Spirit of God, means to be committed to living His way. If you are committed to following Him no matter what the cost, then you are a legitimate son. The struggle or suffering comes when you have to choose to be steadfast in your loyalty to Him and not vacillate in your resolve. This requires discipline, but you don't have to wrestle with this alone. The Spirit will guide you in the right path.

> But the Helper, the Holy Spirit, whom the Father will send in My name, He will teach you all things, and bring to your remembrance all that I said to you.
>
> —JOHN 14:26, NAS

Listen when He speaks to you and obey His instructions. He will show you the way to a higher place in Him.

Chapter 12

WHAT IS THE SPIRIT SAYING TO THE CHURCH?

> For whatever was written in earlier times was written for our instruction, so that through perseverance and the encouragement of the Scriptures we might have hope.
>
> —Romans 15:4, NASB

God called Israel to be a witness and to participate in His great plan of love as it unfolded over thousands of years. The record of their triumphs and failures was written in the Scriptures for instruction and examples to God's people throughout the ages that followed. Through the work of the Cross, God instituted a New Covenant with better promises and mediated by Christ Jesus. (See Heb. 8:6.) Under this New Covenant, the New Testament, the records of Jesus' life, ministry, death, burial, and resurrection were written down to maintain the integrity of God's great plan of love for future generations. God also included teachings on the foundational truths of the New Covenant to train up His New Covenant people as to how they should live.

> All Scripture is inspired by God and profitable for teaching, for reproof, for correction, for training in righteousness; so that the man of God may be adequate, equipped for every good work.
>
> —2 TIMOTHY 3:16–17, NAS

Even as the Law of Moses was given to Israel to train them how to live, the written accounts and personal letters of teaching were given to teach, correct, train, and reprove God's New Covenant people, the Church of the Lord Jesus Christ. The Epistles to the Church addressed the issues of daily living and how Christians were to conduct themselves as members of the Church, the Body of Christ. God wanted to train up His people under the New Covenant so that they could enjoy the great benefits of reconciliation because Jesus, the last Adam, passed the test of commitment and love when He went to the Cross in obedience and fulfillment of God's plan of love.

> So also it is written, "The first MAN, Adam, BECAME A LIVING SOUL." The last Adam became a life-giving spirit.
>
> —1 CORINTHIANS 15:45, NAS

In the Book of Revelation, there occurred a unique situation. The Apostle John transcribed messages for the seven churches of Asia as dictated by Jesus, the Head of the Church. Jesus sent these messages to deal with important issues that needed to be confronted for each local Church. The tone of each message was tempered to the spiritual heart condition of each Church. The spiritual heart condition of the local Church was the sum of the spiritual heart conditions of the members of that Church.

> Saying, "Write in a book what you see, and send it to the seven churches: to Ephesus and to Smyrna and to Pergamum and to Thyatira and to Sardis and to Philadelphia and to Laodicea."
>
> —REVELATION 1:11, NAS

John witnessed Jesus in His risen glory, which caused him to faint at the Lord's feet. As Head of the Church, Jesus came to personally deliver these messages to emphasize their importance to the Body of Christ for that time and for future generations. The issues He dealt with were timeless in their nature and apply to first century believers as well as twenty-first century believers. His purpose was not to condemn and punish, but to uncover the hindrances that were poisoning their relationship with Him. Jesus had given everything on the Cross for the Church, so He brought a message of correction to protect His own from the assault of the enemy who was already within the gates of the Church.

> Husbands, love your wives, just as Christ also loved the Church and gave Himself up for her, so that He might sanctify her, having cleansed her by the washing of water with the word, that He might present to Himself the Church in all her glory, having no spot or wrinkle or any such thing; but that she would be holy and blameless.
>
> —EPHESIANS 5:25–27, NASB

The progressive revelation of God's plan of love had as its ultimate purpose the restoration of man back to intimate fellowship with Himself. When the Holy Spirit came on the Day of Pentecost, the Church of the Lord Jesus Christ was born. The Church was set apart to spread the good news of reconciliation to everyone who would hear and receive the message. God's love for man would now be exposed in the glory that rested upon His New Covenant people, His Church.

The Holy Spirit came to teach and lead the Church to fulfill her commission to be the agents of Christ on earth. The Book of Acts chronicled the birth and growth of the early Church, however, the Holy Spirit's job continued beyond the pages of that book and continues today.

> I will ask the Father, and He will give you another Helper, that He may be with you forever; that is the Spirit of truth, whom the world cannot receive, because it does not see Him or know Him, but you know Him because He abides with you and will be in you.
>
> —JOHN 14:16–17, NASB

God did not come this far to leave the work of His great plan incomplete. He assured the success of His work by sending His Spirit to indwell His people, the Church. Israel did not have the benefit of the indwelling of the Spirit. But, when man was reconciled to God through the sacrifice of the Cross, the Spirit of God was free to indwell those who belonged to Christ (see Acts 17:28). Now it was time to train up these children of God to walk in the fullness of their covenant. As Head of the Church, Jesus addressed the seven churches to instruct them and to convey His approval and disapproval of their actions.

Jesus' messages to the seven churches are just as potent and applicable today as they were when John transcribed them on the Isle of Patmos. Jesus specifically confronts the issues in each local Church that hinders their relationship with Him. These hindrances have a strange familiarity because they also hindered Israel in her walk with God under the Old Covenant, symbolized by the High Places. Since God's ultimate goal is intimate fellowship with His people, He continues to warn and teach about the obstacles to their communion.

> He who has an ear, let him hear what the Spirit says to the churches.
>
> —REVELATION 2:7, NASB

The Spirit is speaking to the Church today corporately and individually. Seek His counsel and He will show you the way you should go to arrive at a higher place in Him.

CHAPTER 13

MESSAGE TO EPHESUS: FIRST LOVE

To the angel of the Church in Ephesus write: The One who holds the seven stars in His right hand, the One who walks among the seven golden lampstands, says this: "I know your deeds and your toil and perseverance, and that you cannot tolerate evil men, and you put to the test those who call themselves apostles, and they are not, and you found them to be false; and you have perseverance and have endured for My name's sake, and have not grown weary. But I have this against you, that you have left your first love. Therefore remember from where you have fallen, and repent and do the deeds you did at first; or else I am coming to you and will remove your lampstand out of its place—unless you repent. Yet this you do have, that you hate the deeds of the Nicolaitans, which I also hate. He who has an ear, let him hear what the Spirit says to the churches. To him who overcomes, I will grant to eat of the tree of life which is in the Paradise of God."

—REVELATION 2:1–7, NASB

The Lord Jesus began His message by reminding the Ephesians that He is the One who holds the Church in His hand. As Head of the Church, Jesus called them to attention, thereby establishing the importance of what He was about to say. The Lord complimented the Ephesians for their current and past deeds. They maintained a standard of holiness by challenging evil and testing and exposing falsehoods in the Church. The Lord acknowledged them for their faithfulness and endurance in the face of many hardships.

However, Jesus confronted a serious problem that existed in the local Church with these words, "But I have this against you, that you have left your first love" (Rev. 2:4). These words of admonishment exposed a spiritual heart condition that was hidden underneath their good works and zeal to stand against false teachers. Jesus came to warn them that works could not replace the need to maintain a personal relationship with Him. He complimented their zeal for the truth, but their love for Him had to be the reason for their actions.

Even as Samuel warned King Saul and the people of Israel about the dangers of becoming enamored with the process of worship instead of who they worshiped, Jesus warned the Ephesians that the source of their works had to come from their love relationship with Him. He reminded this congregation that they had started out correctly. They just needed to return to putting Jesus back as the focus of their lives.

If the Ephesians did not give their love relationship with the Lord first priority, they were heading for the dangerous waters of self-sufficiency. Instead of depending on their love relationship with the Lord to give them direction and purpose, they flirted with self-reliance and an independent attitude. This slippery slope only led to disaster, as Israel's example had shown. A self-sufficient attitude fostered the building of High Places in their hearts and caused them to be prideful and to lightly regard the Word of God.

Jesus sent the Ephesians this personal message because He loved them and wanted them to understand the gravity of the situation. Their personal love relationship with Him was not to be taken lightly. The ultimate goal of God's plan of love was to restore man to a place where he could again enjoy a personal love relationship with God. This was not an afterthought or lagniappe (bonus), but the reason Jesus went to the Cross. God had exposed His loving heart once more to man, but now His Church was able to reciprocate His love and make it the focus of their lives.

Even after His rebuke, Jesus commended the Ephesians for standing against the Nicolaitans. "Yet this you do have, that you hate the deeds of the Nicolaitans, which I also hate." (Rev. 2:6). The Nicolaitans perverted the teachings of Christ for personal gain. Whether it was the manipulation of the Church by self-proclaimed and self-promoted false leaders for profit and power, or the mixing of heathen rituals with those of the Church, the Lord hated their deeds. The Apostle Paul also confronted these deeds in 2 Timothy 4:3–4 and in Titus 1:10–14. By using such strong language, Jesus was proclaiming that such behavior was despicable and not to be tolerated by His people. The Nicolaitans were enemies of the Gospel of Christ and their message was anti-Christ.

> Children, it is the last hour; and just as you heard that antichrist is coming, even now many antichrists have appeared; from this we know that it is the last hour. They went out from us, but they were not really of us; for if they had been of us, they would have remained with us; but they went out, so that it would be shown that they all are not of us.
>
> —1 JOHN 2:18–19, NASB

"He who has an ear, let him hear what the Spirit says to the churches. To him who overcomes, I will grant to eat of the tree of life which is in the Paradise of God," (Rev. 2:7, NAS). Jesus declared that if the Ephesians repented and returned to their first love, as overcomers they would eat of the tree of life. Even as the Lord God continually offered forgiveness to the children of Israel, Jesus was calling His people to stay faithful to Him, as He remained faithful to them.

If good works were the only criteria that qualified a local Church or individual believer as a true follower of Christ, then complete dependence on God would be unnecessary. But, man could not save himself; he needed a Savior, the Sinless One, to pay the price of sin for the sinner. "I [Jesus] am the vine, you are the branches; he who abides in Me and I in him, he bears much fruit, for apart from Me you can do nothing," (John 15:5, NAS). Admitting dependence on the Lord Jesus was the only way the Ephesians could return to their first love and focus on the love of God that wrought such a great plan of salvation.

> And we have such trust through Christ toward God. Not that we are sufficient of ourselves to think of anything as being from ourselves, but our sufficiency is from God, who also made us sufficient as ministers of the new covenant, not of the letter but of the Spirit; for the letter kills, but the Spirit gives life.
>
> —2 CORINTHIANS 3:4–6, NKJV

Everyone who overcomes the practice of doing Christian works out of habit or for the work's sake and returns to their first love, intimate love, with the Lord Jesus, has the promise to eat of the tree of life that is in heaven. This message to the Ephesians transcends time and is a call to every local Church and individual Christian to stay the course and remember the ultimate goal of the sacrifice of the Cross—the restoration of man to enjoy a personal love relationship with God.

Admit your dependence on Him and He will respond to you by taking you to a higher place in Him.

Chapter 14

MESSAGE TO PERGAMUM: NO COMPROMISE

And to the angel of the Church in Pergamum write: The One who has the sharp two-edged sword says this: "I know where you dwell, where Satan's throne is; and you hold fast My name, and did not deny My faith even in the days of Antipas, My witness, My faithful one, who was killed among you, where Satan dwells. But I have a few things against you, because you have there some who hold the teaching of Balaam, who kept teaching Balak to put a stumbling block before the sons of Israel, to eat things sacrificed to idols and to commit acts of immorality. So you also have some who in the same way hold the teaching of the Nicolaitans. Therefore repent; or else I am coming to you quickly, and I will make war against them with the sword of My mouth. He who has an ear, let him hear what the Spirit says to the churches. To him who overcomes, to him I will give some of the hidden manna, and I will give him a white stone, and a new name written on the stone which no one knows but he who receives it."

—Revelation 2:12–17, NASB

The Lord Jesus, Head of the Church, identified Himself as the One who had the two-edged sword. The Word of God is the two-edged sword as described in Hebrews 4:12, "For the word of God is living and active and sharper than any two-edged sword, and piercing as far as the division of soul and spirit, of both joints and marrow, and able to judge the thoughts and intentions of the heart," (NAS). As the Word of God made flesh, Jesus addressed the Church at Pergamum this way to establish His authority and ability to rightly discern their spiritual heart condition.

Jesus commended the Church at Peramum for not denying faith in His name even when some of them were martyred. This Church dwelt in the midst of a corrupt and wicked city; Jesus called it the seat of Satan. Although they were surrounded by wickedness, Jesus acknowledged their faithfulness, especially Antipas who was killed.

However, Jesus proceeded to confront the main issues that concerned Him in Pergamum with these words, "But I have a few things against you." This congregation of believers was tolerating members who practiced the doctrine of Balaam and the teachings of the Nicolaitans. They were compromising within their group, yet standing against the wickedness that was easily identified outside of the Church. Jesus was uncovering this self-deception to call the Church to repentance.

The doctrine of Balaam was given to King Balak of Moab as a plan to corrupt Israel through intermarriage with the women of Moab. (See Num. 31:15–16.) These women were to bring into their marriages the practice of worshiping other gods and turn their husbands away from the Lord God. King Solomon was a prime example of how the doctrine of Balaam could corrupt from within and bring spiritual ruin. The deeds of the Nicolaitans were anti-Christ. Jesus again stated His hatred for them. They were pretenders who preyed on the children of God for profit and gain, and through manipulation set up man-made traditions to maintain their places of power. (See 1 John 2:18–19.)

> Do not be bound together with unbelievers; for what partnership have righteousness and lawlessness, or what fellowship has light with darkness? Or what harmony has Christ with Belial, or what has a believer in common with an unbeliever? Or what agreement has the Temple of God with idols? For we are the Temple of the living God; just as God said, "I WILL DWELL IN THEM AND WALK AMONG THEM; AND I WILL BE THEIR GOD, AND THEY SHALL BE MY PEOPLE. Therefore, COME OUT FROM THEIR MIDST AND BE SEPARATE," says the Lord. "AND DO NOT TOUCH WHAT IS UNCLEAN; and I will welcome you. And I will be a father to you, and you shall be sons and daughters to Me," says the Lord Almighty.
>
> —2 Corinthians 6:14–18, nas

The Church at Pergamum had fallen victim to a fickle heart. They wavered in their commitment to the Word of God within their congregation. They had proven themselves faithful when the evil came from a source outside of the Church; however, they tolerated compromise among the brethren. (See Acts 20:29–30.) This same type of deception was at work among the children of Israel as they proliferated the use of the High Places under the pretext of worshiping the Lord God. Jesus brought His message of admonishment to clearly state that the Church of Pergamum needed to repent and recommit to the standard of His Word. If they did not repent, judgment would swiftly fall.

However, to the ones who did repent and overcame this challenge to their faith, Jesus promised to give them hidden manna and an engraved white stone. The hidden manna was a promise of provision for their needs and great personal blessings. The engraved white stone represented a personal gift from the Lord. Each overcomer's gift was engraved with a new name given to them as a sign of intimate affection. Throughout the Bible, God gave new names to people as an open sign of His affection and purpose in their lives. Abram became Abraham; Jacob became Israel; Saul of Tarsus became Paul, the Apostle. Isaiah declared that God would rename Israel.

> The nations will see your righteousness, and all kings your glory; and you will be called by a new name which the mouth of the LORD will designate.
>
> —ISAIAH 62:2, NASB

Although the Church at Pergamum had manifested a fickle heart, Jesus offered great blessings to them if they repented, thereby returning to the truth. His great love for His Church was evident even in His rebuke. The engraved white stone, His personal gift to the overcomer, revealed the depth of His love. A blood covenant required each party to take on the name, assets, and/or debts of the other party. By assuming the sinner's name, Jesus took on the name and debts of the sinner and stood in the sinner's place. On the Cross He paid the debt for the sinner. The overcomer, by receiving Jesus as Lord, took on His name and the benefits that belonged to Him. This promise was not only for the Church at Pergamum, but also for every Christian throughout the ages.

> For the time will come when they will not endure sound doctrine, but according to their own desires, because they have itching ears, they will heap up for themselves teachers; and they will turn their ears away from the truth, and be turned aside to fables.
>
> —2 TIMOTHY 4:3–4, NKJV

The opportunities to compromise our Christian values present themselves everyday. Compromise is promoted by the worldly system because it does not believe in the absolutes established by God. God's gift of free will allows man to choose compromise, but it is unprofitable and destructive. However, even if we have compromised, Jesus offers great blessings to the overcomer who will return to the truth of His Word and recommit to Him.

Enjoy the advantages of your Blood Covenant with the Lord, which gives you access to a higher place in Him.

CHAPTER 15

MESSAGE TO THYATIRA: SPIRITUAL HEART CHECKUP

> And to the angel of the Church in Thyatira write: The Son of God, who has eyes like a flame of fire, and His feet are like burnished bronze, says this: "I know your deeds, and your love and faith and service and perseverance, and that your deeds of late are greater than at first. But I have this against you, that you tolerate the woman Jezebel, who calls herself a prophetess, and she teaches and leads My bond-servants astray so that they commit acts of immorality and eat things sacrificed to idols. I gave her time to repent, and she does not want to repent of her immorality. Behold, I will throw her on a bed of sickness, and those who commit adultery with her into great tribulation, unless they repent of her deeds. And I will kill her children with pestilence, and all the churches will know that I am He who searches the minds and hearts; and I will give to each one of you according to your deeds. But I say to you, the rest who are in Thyatira, who do not hold this teaching, who have not known the deep things of Satan, as they call them—I place no other burden on you. Nevertheless what you have, hold fast until I come. He who overcomes, and he who keeps My deeds until the end, TO HIM I WILL GIVE AUTHORITY OVER THE NATIONS; AND HE SHALL RULE THEM WITH

> A ROD OF IRON, AS THE VESSELS OF THE POTTER ARE BROKEN TO PIECES, as I also have received authority from My Father; and I will give him the morning star. He who has an ear, let him hear what the Spirit says to the churches."
>
> —REVELATION 2:18–29, NASB

Jesus, the Head of the Church, identified Himself as the One whose eyes are like blazing fire. When the Lord God sent Elijah to challenge the false gods of Ahab and Jezebel and to call the people of Samaria back to God, He answered Elijah's prayer by sending fire from heaven to consume the sacrifice. (See 1 Kings 18:20–40.) In a similar way, Jesus established Himself as the fire from heaven that had come to instruct the Church of Thyatira. Jesus praised the Thyatirans for their works, love, faith, service, and endurance. He commended them for expanding these endeavors and doing more than when they first started.

However, there were issues to be confronted that were affecting their spiritual heart condition. The Church at Thyatira was allowing a false prophetess to teach and mislead the people of God into sin. Jesus called her Jezebel to uncover the spirit behind her actions. Even as wicked Queen Jezebel manipulated and goaded King Ahab of Samaria into deep Baal worship, so was this false prophetess doing a similar thing in the Church at Thyatira. Jesus rebuked the congregation for not challenging her like the Ephesians did to the false prophets who came to their Church.

Jesus revealed that He had been dealing with this issue in their Church, because He had given this woman time to repent of her ways. That meant she had been warned, whether privately or publicly or both, however she did not repent and continued spreading her evil among the brethren. Judgment was going to fall on her and her followers and Jesus wanted the Thyatirans to know that He was the source of the calamity because she was hurting His Church. (See Prov. 1:25–27.)

> I the Lord search the heart and examine the mind, to reward a man according to his conduct, according to what his deeds deserve.
>
> —JEREMIAH 17:10, NIV

Jesus searched the hearts of this congregation and knew who had openly followed the false prophetess and who had followed her secretly. Their deeds were known to Him and could not be hidden because He read their hearts with His "eyes like a flame of fire." This declaration informed the Thyatirans it was time for a spiritual heart checkup. If they had stumbled by following this woman, it was time to repent. This was serious business, which was conveyed by the Lord's strong language. Jesus gave His life for the Church and His passion for her welfare was like a blazing fire.

Jesus acknowledged that there were some in Thyatira who did not follow the false prophetess. This meant that there was conflict in the Church of Thyatira between the followers of the false prophetess and the remnant who held fast to the teachings of Christ. Jesus commended the remnant of true believers to continue with what they were doing and to maintain their devotion to Him and the truth.

The Lord gave a promise to the one who overcame the false teachings of Jezebel that they were to rule the nations with a rod of iron. The overcoming Christian would judge the nations and rule as the Lord directs. He then promised them the "Morning Star."

> I, Jesus, have sent *My* angel to testify to you these things for the churches. I am the root and the descendant of David, the bright morning star.
>
> —REVELATION 22:16, NASB

One of the issues that the Lord made in this message was that the Thyatirans did not challenge the false teacher when she came as one of the brethren. They should have tested her teachings by going to the scripture and searching out the truth or falsehood of her words. In effect they should have given her a spiritual heart checkup to establish whether she was a true teacher or a false teacher. (See 1 John 4:1; Jude 4.)

You are to guard your hearts today, just as the Thyatirans should have guarded their hearts long ago. Always apply the measuring rod of the Scriptures to any teaching you hear in Church, on the radio, on television, or read in a book—including this one. The Holy Spirit is revealing great things to the Church today, but He will never conflict with the written Word of God. When you hear something that the Word of God does not support then you should question it and seek the Lord about the issue in prayer. Do not condemn your brother, but pray for him that the truth of the Lord be revealed to him and to you concerning this matter.

Submission to the Word of God as your standard for living will profit you in all areas of your life. It is the way that you can openly demonstrate your love for the Lord and keeps your heart teachable. "Jesus replied, 'If anyone loves me, he will obey my teaching. My Father will love him, and we will come to him and make our home with him. He who does not love me will not obey my teaching. These words you hear are not my own; they belong to the Father who sent me,'" (John 14:23–24, NIV).

This message also reveals the depth of passion that the Lord has for His Church. Even as a protective parent fights against anyone who would harm his family, so does the Lord Jesus protect and guard His Church. The Good Shepherd willingly lays down His life for the sheep. He will fight the enemy, who comes as a roaring lion that tries to devour and deceive His people with false teachings and man-made traditions. His great plan of love cannot be thwarted and He will watch over His people with an unquenchable zeal.

Let the Holy Spirit enlighten you about His great love for you and His desire to take you to a higher place in Him. Let His Word be your measuring stick as you give yourself a spiritual heart checkup.

CHAPTER 16

MESSAGE TO SARDIS: WAKE UP

To the angel of the Church in Sardis write: He who has the seven Spirits of God and the seven stars, says this: "I know your deeds, that you have a name that you are alive, but you are dead. Wake up, and strengthen the things that remain, which were about to die; for I have not found your deeds completed in the sight of My God. So remember what you have received and heard; and keep it, and repent. Therefore if you do not wake up, I will come like a thief, and you will not know at what hour I will come to you. But you have a few people in Sardis who have not soiled their garments; and they will walk with Me in white, for they are worthy. He who overcomes will thus be clothed in white garments; and I will not erase his name from the book of life, and I will confess his name before My Father and before His angels. He who has an ear, let him hear what the Spirit says to the churches."

—REVELATION 3:1–6, NASB

Jesus, the Head of the Church, identified Himself as the One who has the seven spirits of God and the seven stars. The seven stars were identified as the seven angels, or messengers, of the seven churches of Asia and the seven spirits were those which were before the Throne of God in heaven. (See Rev. 1:4.) This description established Jesus as speaking from the Throne of God in agreement with the Father and the Holy Spirit.

Unlike the previous churches Jesus did not commend the Church in Sardis for anything. His words were sharp and corrective. The Church of Sardis had a reputation, with men, for being spiritually alive, but the Lord told them they were actually spiritually dead. He called them to "wake up." Just as the dying embers of a fire can be stirred to life by blowing on them, Jesus called the Sardis Church to stir up the dying embers of their faith in Him.

> Are you so foolish? Having begun by the Spirit, are you now being perfected by the flesh? Did you suffer so many things in vain—if indeed it was in vain? So then, does He who provides you with the Spirit and works miracles among you, do it by the works of the Law, or by hearing with faith?
>
> —GALATIANS 3:3–5, NASB

> For in Christ Jesus neither circumcision nor uncircumcision means anything, but faith working through love.
>
> —GALATIANS 5:6, NASB

> Even so faith, if it has no works, is dead, being by itself. But someone may well say, "You have faith and I have works; show me your faith without the works, and I will show you my faith by my works." You believe that God is one. You do well; the demons also believe, and shudder. But are you willing to recognize, you foolish fellow, that faith without works is useless?
>
> —JAMES 2:17–20, NAS

These scriptures in Galatians and James testified to the source of the Sardis Church's problem. The Law could not save them; it was only meant to point the People of God to the Messiah. Only active faith in Jesus Christ was the guarantee of their salvation. Faith has to work through love to be effective. However, faith has to produce works, or evidence of salvation, to be alive. Faith without the evidence of good works, or fruit, is dead. (See John 15:5.)

Sardis had a reputation of being alive spiritually, so at one time they had been. However, at the time of this message Jesus indicated that He did not find their works to be complete. This stern rebuke indicated that Sardis was not operating in active faith or in love because they were not pleasing the Lord. (See Heb. 11:6.) Jesus also testified that the Church of Sardis had been taught the truth; they knew better. They had to repent for being unteachable, disobedient, and rebellious. A disobedient and unteachable heart was one of the High Place stumbling blocks that had hindered Israel's walk with the Lord God.

The parable of the sower and the seed revealed a similar spiritual heart condition to the one in Sardis. "Other seed fell among the thorns, and the thorns came up and choked it, and it yielded no crop" (Mark 4:7, NASB). These were the ones who allowed the worries and cares of this world to choke the Word of God and keep it from producing fruit in their lives. Sardis received a wake up call because she did not even realize her true spiritual condition.

The Lord Jesus recognized the fact that there was a remnant in Sardis who were still alive in faith and operating in love. (See Heb. 11:6.) He commended them by calling them worthy and acknowledged that their garments were unstained and white. These garments were their garments of salvation. The garments of the Bride of Christ are identified in Revelation 19:8 as the, "righteous acts of the saints." The Lord said He would declare the names of those who overcame the challenge to their faith before the Father and the angels in heaven.

"So do not worry about tomorrow; for tomorrow will care for itself. Each day has enough trouble of its own," (Matt. 6:34, NASB). Jesus knows that the cares of everyday life can be a cruel taskmaster. His words of instruction were written down so that they can continue to teach His people throughout the ages. That is why it is vitally important for every Christian to read and study the Word of God. Jesus' words are just as timely and relevant as when He first spoke them. They are powerful and filled with love. The Holy Spirit brings the light of revelation when you turn to the Word of God for direction and comfort.

> Ask, and it will be given to you; seek, and you will find; knock, and it will be opened to you. For everyone who asks receives, and he who seeks finds, and to him who knocks it will be opened. Or what man is there among you who, when his son asks for a loaf, will give him a stone? Or if he asks for a fish, he will not give him a snake, will he? If you then, being evil, know how to give good gifts to your children, how much more will your Father who is in heaven give what is good to those who ask Him!
>
> —Matthew 7:7–11, NASB

The Lord is looking for you to give Him top priority in your life. This is the key to achieving a higher place in Him. Ask Him to come into your life, and experience the joy He brings.

Chapter 17

MESSAGE TO LAODICEA: DON'T BE LUKEWARM

To the angel of the Church in Laodicea write: The Amen, the faithful and true Witness, the Beginning of the creation of God, says this: "I know your deeds, that you are neither cold nor hot; I wish that you were cold or hot. So because you are lukewarm, and neither hot nor cold, I will spit you out of My mouth. Because you say, "I am rich, and have become wealthy, and have need of nothing,' and you do not know that you are wretched and miserable and poor and blind and naked, I advise you to buy from Me gold refined by fire so that you may become rich, and white garments so that you may clothe yourself, and that the shame of your nakedness will not be revealed; and eye salve to anoint your eyes so that you may see. Those whom I love, I reprove and discipline; therefore be zealous and repent. Behold, I stand at the door and knock; if anyone hears My voice and opens the door, I will come in to him and will dine with him, and he with Me. He who overcomes, I will grant to him to sit down with Me on My throne, as I also overcame and sat down with My Father on His throne. He who has an ear, let him hear what the Spirit says to the churches."

—Revelation 3:14–22, NASB

Jesus, the Head of the Church, identified Himself as the Amen, the faithful and true Witness, and the Beginning of creation. Jesus established that His words to the Laodiceans were the testimony of the spiritual condition of their congregation. Jesus confirmed His position as the faithful Witness as the Beginning of creation—The Alpha.

Like the Church of Sardis, Jesus had no words of commendation for the Laodiceans. He said that He knew their works and found them to be lukewarm. The term "lukewarm" indicated that the Laodiceans were indifferent and halfhearted in their association with the Lord. This halfhearted attitude repulsed Jesus to the point where He said He would spit them out of His mouth.

The Laodiceans had fallen prey to a self-sufficient attitude and mentality. They had said in their hearts that they were satisfied with their wealth and goods and needed nothing else, which included the Lord. This was the same sort of mind-set that caused Israel to elevate their will, opinions, and culture above the Law of God as symbolized by the High Places. Just like Israel, the Laodiceans had forgotten Who was the source of their blessings and the high cost that He paid for their freedom from sin.

Jesus rebuked the Laodiceans with very strong language to shake them out of their indifference. The True Witness told the Church of Laodicea that they were really wretched, miserable, poor, blind, and naked. Their priorities were askew and their lifestyle was out of control. But, the Lord did not just reprimand them, He counseled them to come to Him and buy gold that was tried in fire. Jesus was speaking about their faith, which is more precious than gold. The white garments He offered to them to cover their nakedness were the garments of salvation—the righteousness of the saints.

> So that the proof of your faith, being more precious than gold which is perishable, even though tested by fire, may be found to result in praise and glory and

> honor at the revelation of Jesus Christ.
>
> —1 PETER 1:7, NASB

Jesus called the Laodiceans to repent of their complacency and return to Him. He was ready to make them rich through the trial of their faith, which is worth more than earthly gold. He was ready and willing to cover their nakedness with the garments of salvation. He was able to open their eyes with spiritual revelation so that they would comprehend the truth. Jesus told the Laodiceans that His love for them was the reason for His rebuke. He was contending for their hearts even as the Lord God had spoken to Israel through the prophet Isaiah.

> Learn to do good; Seek justice, Reprove the ruthless; Defend the orphan, Plead for the widow. "Come now, and let us reason together," Says the LORD, "Though your sins are as scarlet, They will be as white as snow; Though they are red like crimson, They will be like wool. If you consent and obey, You will eat the best of the land."
>
> —ISAIAH 1:17–19, NAS

Jesus revealed the greatness of His love when He told the Laodiceans that even their indifference to Him had not cooled His passion for them. He told them that He stood at the door and knocked calling out to whoever would listen to open the door of their heart. If they responded, He would come in and sup with them. This indicated the intimate way Jesus wanted to commune with the Laodiceans—fellowship around the Table of the Lord.

The overcomer was promised to sit with Jesus in His Throne. Although this was first spoken to the Laodicean Church, Jesus made this offer to His Church throughout the ages. Even the lukewarm Laodiceans were given the promise to sit with Jesus at the very Throne of God, if they returned to Him. God's mercy and grace are evident even in this rebuke-filled message.

> Ho! Every one who thirsts, come to the waters; And you who have no money come, buy and eat. Come, buy wine and milk without money and without cost.
>
> —ISAIAH 55:1, NAS

Self-reliance is not an asset for a Christian from God's perspective. It blocks the Christian from receiving anything from the Lord because he looks to himself first as the source of strength. Natural strengths and talents are no match to what the Lord has to offer the one who learns to turn to Him first and depend on Him alone. (See Dan. 3.)

> "For My thoughts are not your thoughts, nor are your ways My ways," declares the LORD. "For as the heavens are higher than the earth, so are My ways higher than your ways and My thoughts than your thoughts."
>
> —ISAIAH 55:8–9, NASB

After considering the full message to the Church of Laodicea, there is no reason to fear a personal spiritual assessment. With the Holy Spirit's direction, you can only achieve victory and great rewards. However, the best part of drawing closer to the Lord is the wonderful opportunity of an intimate relationship with Him. You will never be disappointed because you can never out-love Him.

> I sought Your favor with all my heart; be gracious to me according to Your word. I considered my ways and turned my feet to Your testimonies. I hastened and did not delay to keep Your commandments.
>
> —PSALMS 119:58–60, NASB

True success and prosperity can only come when you admit your total dependence on God and allow Him to draw you to a higher place in Him.

CHAPTER 18

MESSAGES TO SMYRNA AND PHILADELPHIA: ENCOURAGEMENT AND APPROVAL

> And to the angel of the Church in Smyrna write: The first and the last, who was dead, and has come to life, says this: "I know your tribulation and your poverty (but you are rich), and the blasphemy by those who say they are Jews and are not, but are a synagogue of Satan. Do not fear what you are about to suffer. Behold, the devil is about to cast some of you into prison, so that you will be tested, and you will have tribulation for ten days. Be faithful until death, and I will give you the crown of life. He who has an ear, let him hear what the Spirit says to the churches. He who overcomes will not be hurt by the second death."
>
> —REVELATION 2:8–11, NASB

Jesus, the Head of the Church, identified Himself as the First and the Last, who was dead and has come to life. These words were meant to instill confidence in the Smyrna Christians that the One who was watching over them will never leave them.

Jesus had only praise for the Church of Smyrna. He commended them for their works and endurance through tribulations and persecutions. "Behold, I have refined you, but not as silver; I have tested you in the furnace of affliction," (Isa. 48:10, NAS). Their faith, which was proven in the fires of affliction, was their great treasure from Jesus' perspective.

Jesus prophesied to this Church about the coming imprisonment and sufferings they would encounter. The ten days were ten seasons of persecution, however, the Lord comforted them by assuring them that He would give them the Crown of Life.

Jesus promised the overcomer of afflictions and imprisonment that he would never see the second death—eternal separation from God. This wonderful promise was issued by the Head of the Church and has never been withdrawn.

> And to the angel of the Church in Philadelphia write: He who is holy, who is true, who has the key of David, who opens and no one will shut, and who shuts and no one opens, says this: "I know your deeds. Behold, I have put before you an open door which no one can shut, because you have a little power, and have kept My word, and have not denied My name. Behold, I will cause those of the synagogue of Satan, who say that they are Jews and are not, but lie—I will make them come and bow down at your feet, and make them know that I have loved you. Because you have kept the word of My perseverance, I also will keep you from the hour of testing, that hour which is about to come upon the whole world, to test those who dwell on the earth. I am coming quickly; hold fast what you have, so that no one will take your crown. He who overcomes, I will make him a pillar in the Temple of My God, and he will not

> go out from it anymore; and I will write on him the name of My God, and the name of the city of My God, the new Jerusalem, which comes down out of heaven from My God, and My new name. He who has an ear, let him hear what the Spirit says to the churches."
>
> —REVELATION 3:7–13, NASB

Jesus identified Himself as the holy and true One who has the key of David: if He opens no man can shut, if He shuts no man can open. Jesus established the fact that He was in control and the churches were accountable to Him. He knew the Philadelphians' deeds because He watched them, as He continues to watch His Church today. Jesus' assertion of His holiness revealed His Church was called to be holy, even as Israel was called to be holy. When His watchful eyes found churches and individuals whose hearts are perfect towards Him, He fulfilled His promise to show Himself strong on their behalf. (See 2 Chron. 16:9.)

> And I will clothe him with your tunic, and tie your sash securely about him, I will entrust him with your authority, and he will become a father to the inhabitants of Jerusalem and to the house of Judah. Then I will set the key of the house of David on his shoulder, when he opens no one will shut, when he shuts no one will open.
>
> —ISAIAH 22:21–22, NAS

Jesus commended the Philadelphian Church for their works and revealed to them that He opened a door for them that no man could shut. He possessed the key of the house of David and used it on their behalf. Although the Philadelphians had a little strength, they used all they had to keep the commandments of the Lord. Because of their faithfulness and dedication, Jesus promised to make their enemies come worship before them. Through their patience and loyalty they received the Lord's pledge that they would escape the hour of temptation that will come upon the entire world.

> But since we are of the day, let us be sober, having put on the breastplate of faith and love, and as a helmet, the hope of salvation. For God has not destined us for wrath, but for obtaining salvation through our Lord Jesus Christ, who died for us, so that whether we are awake or asleep, we will live together with Him. Therefore encourage one another and build up one another, just as you also are doing.
>
> —1 THESSALONIANS 5:8–11, NAS

To the overcomer, Jesus continued to promise wonderful things. They will be established as a pillar, part of the foundational support of the very Temple of God. He will place His name on them and the name of the New Jerusalem. This signage indicated the Lord's approval and willingness to be identified with His overcoming people. This promise was first made to the Philadelphians, but was meant to call out to the Church throughout the ages of time.

The churches at Smyrna and Philadelphia were examples of tried and tested Christians who kept their commitment of love to God even through trials and persecutions. Their love, devotion, and works came from their love of God and adherence to the commands of Jesus under the New Covenant sealed in His blood. These dear brethren set an example for all Christians to follow throughout the ages.

Hindrances, such as the cares of daily life and the tribulations of living in a corrupt and lost world, will raise obstacles along the way as you endeavor to establish an intimate love relationship with the Lord. But, you are not in this alone; the Lord is kind and merciful. He is always ready to fellowship with you. He stands at the door of your heart, knocking and calling out to you to let Him in. He pursues you and contends for your love and affection. The sacrifice of the Cross has made this possible and He seeks every opportunity to invite you into His presence.

> Come to Me, all who are weary and heavy-laden, and I will give you rest. Take My yoke upon you and learn from Me, for I am gentle and humble in heart, and YOU WILL FIND REST FOR YOUR SOULS. For My yoke is easy and My burden is light.
>
> —MATTHEW 11:28–30, NASB

In His presence He can reveal the deep things of His heart to you as you dwell in a higher place in Him. He can teach you how to live and be strong in the power of His might and to overcome every obstacle. He can bless you and enable you to be a blessing to others.

Chapter 19

THE HOLY SPIRIT'S JOB

So then, my beloved, just as you have always obeyed, not as in my presence only, but now much more in my absence, work out your salvation with fear and trembling; for it is God who is at work in you, both to will and to work for His good pleasure.

—Philippians 2:12–13, nas

This scripture reveals the need for every Christian to work out his salvation. The work part involves establishing a love relationship with the Lord. A relationship between two individuals requires an investment of time and energy from both parties. This is true whether the relationship is between a child and his parent, a husband and wife, or a believer and the Lord. Even as natural relationships mature and develop, a believer's relationship with the Lord must grow and deepen over time. This relationship needs to be nurtured by spending time in His presence and getting to know the Lord through His written Word and prayer.

Therefore I urge you, brethren, by the mercies of God, to present your bodies a living and holy sacrifice,

> acceptable to God, which is your spiritual service of worship. And do not be conformed to this world, but be transformed by the renewing of your mind, so that you may prove what the will of God is, that which is good and acceptable and perfect.
>
> —ROMANS 12:1–2, NASB

The Apostle Paul, in his letters to the Philippians and Romans, instructs Christians to work out their own salvation, and to renew their minds. Believers are responsible for their thinking, acting, conversation, and the way they live before God and man. When a person is born again his spirit is reborn, indwelt and made alive by the Spirit of God, however, his mind is in need of renewal. Only developing and maturing a deep, intimate, personal relationship with God can accomplish the process of renewing the mind.

The goal of God's great plan of love is to restore man back to his original state of being able to have an intimate relationship with Him. This work is to be approached with reverential awe of a merciful and gracious God whose love for mankind is spoken through the Cross. But His great plan does not stop there, He sent the Holy Spirit to indwell those who receive His offer of salvation and love. The very Spirit of God lives in each believer to accomplish the work of renewal so that intimate communion with God can be accomplished. "For it is God who is at work in you, both to will and to work for His good pleasure" (Phil. 2:13, NAS).

> I will ask the Father, and He will give you another Helper, that He may be with you forever; that is the Spirit of truth, whom the world cannot receive, because it does not see Him or know Him, but you know Him because He abides with you and will be in you.
>
> —JOHN 14:16–17, NASB

Although the Holy Spirit lives within the believer, He does not take away his free will. This free will sets man apart from all other earth creatures. It makes it possible for man to have a true love relationship with the Lord and to reject Him as well. Each believer must personally respond to the Lord's invitation of intimacy, and then the Holy Spirit can assist him in the work of building a relationship with God. The Holy Spirit's work is vital to every believer because without His indwelling presence it would be impossible to overcome the hindrances that can block his communion with the Lord. God's mercy and compassion are revealed through His provision of so great a Comforter.

> But when He, the Spirit of truth, comes, He will guide you into all the truth; for He will not speak on His own initiative, but whatever He hears, He will speak; and He will disclose to you what is to come. He will glorify Me, for He will take of Mine and will disclose it to you. All things that the Father has are Mine; therefore I said that He takes of Mine and will disclose it to you.
>
> —JOHN 16:13–15, NASB

The Word says that the Holy Spirit's job is to reveal Jesus to the Christian. The Cross is Jesus' commitment to the world: an open proposal for whosoever will believe in Him. When a person receives Jesus as Savior, he pledges himself to the Lord and declares his acceptance of the Lord's invitation to intimately fellowship with Him. This relationship grows as the believer comes to know the Lord through His Word, through prayer, through the communion table, through his brothers and sisters in the Church, and especially through the revealing ministry of the Spirit in his life.

This relationship progresses like the blossoming of a lovely rose. As the rose matures, it opens layer after layer releasing a beautiful fragrance as more and more beauty is revealed. The bud contains all of the beauty of the rose, but it is only in the potential form. Looking at the bud, you must see with the eyes of faith knowing that the beauty of the rose within will soon explode into view. Finally, the full flower displays the complete magnificence of the rose.

Our relationship with the Lord is in a continual process of blooming. Unlike the rose, the unfolding of higher levels of this relationship depends on our willingness to seek His face and His presence. There are obstacles to overcome to achieve the fullness of our covenant relationship with the Lord, which can rise up within our hearts and cause us to stumble.

> Watch over your heart with all diligence, for from it flow the springs of life.
>
> —PROVERBS 4:23, NAS

Here is another place where the Word instructs us to take God-directed action as part of our responsibility in our relationship with the Lord. If we are instructed to watch over our hearts with diligence there must be an enemy to guard against. If we are not careful, then High Places can be established within our hearts that will choke off the springs of life in us. High Places of the heart will hinder the Holy Spirit's work in us.

There are three important things to do in order to guard our hearts from establishing High Places that exalt themselves above the knowledge of God. (See 2 Cor. 10:3–5.) First, we must *admit* that we need the Lord and can do nothing of eternal worth without Him. Second, we must *submit* to His Lordship and keep our hearts teachable and obedient. Finally, we must *commit* to following His instructions no matter where they lead us.

The Holy Spirit's job is to help you do these things in your life. Let Him bring you closer to the Lord than ever before as you learn to live in a higher place in Him.

CHAPTER 20

LORD, I NEED YOU

> Not that we are sufficient of ourselves to think of anything as being from ourselves, but our sufficiency is from God.
>
> —2 CORINTHIANS 3:5, NKJV

The dangers of a self-sufficient, independent mind-set toward the things of God were explored by looking at the example of Israel and the Lord's messages to the churches of Asia. This type of thinking caused problems for Israel and the churches and hindered their relationship with God. Israel's use of the High Places symbolized this self-sufficient, unteachable, and fickle spiritual heart condition in an overt manner. However, the true problem was the High Places of the heart that were raised up within the hearts of the people of Israel and the congregations of the churches in Asia.

The Apostle Paul instructs all Christians that their sufficiency is from God. A believer's relationship with the Lord must be centered on admitting that he needs Him. The word admit means to acknowledge, avow, declare openly as fact, to testify, or affirm the truth. Natural human wisdom and strength are not the answer. Only by admitting total dependence on Him and the Covenant of the Cross, can believers establish the foundation of a true love relationship with the Lord.

A believer must also admit when he has made mistakes. God cannot forgive him if he does not repent, and he cannot repent without admitting his error. A prideful heart that cannot admit failure seeks to justify every action. This residue from man's prideful sin nature can insidiously affect the believer's relationship with God.

> I am the vine, you are the branches; he who abides in Me and I in him, he bears much fruit, for apart from Me you can do nothing.
>
> —JOHN 15:5, NAS

The Lord Jesus says that without Him believers can do nothing: nothing of any spiritual value. Their relationship with Him must be one of total dependence. To the unrenewed natural mind this sounds like mind control, but the Lord never takes away man's free will. He created man to be free to choose Him and to seek Him of his own heart's desire. If people were preprogrammed to love the Lord and had no choice in the matter, then their relationship with Him would be superficial and hollow.

Because God gave man free will, man must freely admit that without the Lord he can do nothing. Just like the branch needs the vine to exist, so is the believer's relationship with the Lord. The vine distributes its life force to the entire plant. The branch is attached to the vine and draws the nutrients it needs non-stop, twenty-four hours a day from the vine. The branch is the place where fruit is produced and needs the nutrients from the vine to fulfill its destiny. It continually draws nourishment from the vine, nourishment that is freely given, and goes about its business of producing fruit. It is a wonderful arrangement for the branch and the vine.

> I am the true vine, and My Father is the vinedresser. Every branch in Me that does not bear fruit, He takes away; and every branch that bears fruit, He prunes it so that it may bear more fruit. You are already clean because of the word which I have spoken to you. Abide in Me, and I in you. As the branch cannot bear fruit of itself unless it abides in the vine, so neither can you unless you abide in Me. I am the vine, you are the branches; he who abides in Me and I in him, he bears much fruit, for apart from Me you can do nothing. If anyone does not abide in Me, he is thrown away as a branch and dries up; and they gather them, and cast them into the fire and they are burned. If you abide in Me, and My words abide in you, ask whatever you wish, and it will be done for you.
>
> —JOHN 15:1–7, NAS

Jesus identifies Himself as the vine, the true vine, and God, the Father, as the vinedresser, or farmer. Every unproductive, nonfruit-bearing branch is cut away by the vinedresser. Every fruit-bearing branch is pruned so that it will produce more fruit. There is an ongoing relationship-building process, whereby the vinedresser tends to the branches of the vine to keep it flourishing and producing fruit. Jesus likens his disciples to pruned branches and the pruning implement is the Word of God. (See Heb. 4:12.) The Word of God, the two-edged sword, has pruning qualities to discern between the thoughts and intents of the human heart.

"Abide in Me, and I in you" (John 15:4). The implied subject of Jesus' statement is "you." "You" must choose to abide. In the natural world, a branch has no choice whether to be joined to the vine or not. The spiritual branch (the believer) has a choice to make: will he choose to abide in the vine, Christ, or not. The Lord's statement indicates that the believer has the responsibility to choose to abide in Him and it is a prerequisite to His abidance in the believer. However, the Lord continually stands at the door of every heart knocking and calling out to whomever will listen with words of love and acceptance. He does not bully His way into your heart, but He ardently pursues every man, woman, and child because of His great love.

A person can choose to reject His offer of love and not abide in the vine of life. He is like the branch that is cut off from the vine. But, through the wonderful process of repentance and rededication he can be restored, or grafted back on, to the spiritual vine, the Lord Jesus Christ. The abider in the spiritual vine is given a great promise, "If you abide in Me, and My words abide in you, ask whatever you wish, and it will be done for you" (John 15:7). This promise assures the abider that his prayers will be answered. However, because he is abiding in the Lord, he will only ask for things in agreement with the will and Word of God.

Therefore, in order to tear down the High Place of a self-sufficient and self-reliant attitude, it is necessary to admit total dependence on the Lord in every area of our lives. It is also necessary to admit failure without excuse, repent, and ask for forgiveness whenever sin separates us from the vine, the Lord. "Lord, I need you," should be the cry from the lips of every child of God. Through the progressive revelation of His great love, the Lord has provided a way for His people to be reinstated to intimate fellowship with Him and to continue to be restored after every failure.

> There is no fear in love; but perfect love casts out fear, because fear involves punishment, and the one who fears is not perfected in love. We love, because He first loved us.
>
> —1 JOHN 4:18–19, NAS

We love Him because He first loved us. The sacrifice of the Cross demonstrates that love for eternity. To think or act as though we can save ourselves effectively rebuffs His sacrifice as being unnecessary. The reason this type of attitude blocks us from an intimate love relationship with God is that it marginalizes His great plan of love and exalts human capabilities.

Let us realize the wonderfulness of His great love and accept our branch-like dependence on Him for our very existence as we learn to love in a higher place in Him.

Lord, I need you. Lord, I love you, because You first loved me.

CHAPTER 21

LORD, I'LL DO IT YOUR WAY

> And do not present your members as instruments of unrighteousness to sin, but present yourselves to God as being alive from the dead, and your members as instruments of righteousness to God.
>
> —ROMANS 6:13, NKJV

The believer has responsibilities and his own contributions to make in establishing an intimate love relationship with God. He needs to guard his heart by admitting that he needs the Lord in every area of his life. Then he needs to learn how to submit his life and ways to the Lord's authority. It becomes a matter of yielding his human will, ideas, plans, and thoughts to the authority of Jesus Christ. In the absence of submission, the High Place of rebellion and stubbornness rises up and hinders his relationship with the Lord.

Submission is not the same thing as agreement. Submission is the cornerstone of the military's chain of command. Those who are positioned under a ranking officer's command must follow his orders. When a command is given, there is no open forum held to discuss the merits of the command or whether the soldiers are in agreement with the order. The soldiers who were issued the orders are expected to follow them without question. This is considered their reasonable service.

God established the concept of chain of command. The angels in heaven are ordered in rank under the leadership of the Lord of Hosts, Jesus, who is also the Head of the Church. Because the Lord operates through the chain of command, He can delegate His authority to those who are fully submitted to it.

Unless a believer has admitted that without the Lord he can do nothing, he cannot submit to the Word of God when conflict arises between his own natural desires and the commands of God. Only when this conflict exists is there evidence of submission. Otherwise the believer may only be in agreement with the Word of God. The voice of true submission says, "I will believe the Word of God is true and will choose to follow it no matter what conflicting thoughts or desires rise up within me."

> Submit therefore to God. Resist the devil and he will flee from you. Draw near to God and He will draw near to you. Cleanse your hands, you sinners; and purify your hearts, you double-minded. Be miserable and mourn and weep; let your laughter be turned into mourning and your joy to gloom. Humble yourselves in the presence of the Lord, and He will exalt you.
>
> —JAMES 4:7–10, NAS

The implied subject of the first statement, "Submit therefore to God," is "you." "You" must choose to submit to God's Word and His will, and then "you" must resist the devil. Only the submitted believer can resist the devil and have God's guarantee that the devil will flee from him. The submitted believer is exercising the authority of Jesus over the devil by His delegation through the chain of command.

Jesus is the believer's example of a totally submitted life. He does not ask His people to do something He was not willing to do. The agony of Jesus in the Garden of Gethsemane displays a struggle of submission between the natural human will and the will of God. The battlefield where the human will struggles with the will of God is in the mind of man. Jesus showed the way when He humbled Himself in obedience to the will of the Father. Because of His obedience as unto death, He has received a name above every name.

The Apostle James instructs the believer to draw near to God and in like fashion God draws near to the believer. When the Lord draws near He brings the comfort of His presence and a multitude of other blessings that abound from His great heart of love. James continues to instruct the believer to take action by cleansing his hands and purifying his heart. The task is accomplished through the pruning work of the Word of God. When there is need for true, heartfelt repentance, the believer is afforded this grace through the Blood of Jesus. God sees the heart and knows the difference between feigned regret for being caught and true godly repentance and sorrow for sinning. A believer experiences true spiritual sorrow and heartfelt shame when it arises from a heart of love for failing his merciful and loving Father.

Humility, submission, and repentance in the sight of the Lord will cause the believer to be lifted up. God responds to these actions by forgiving, comforting, and lifting up the heads of His people. Even as the Lord Jesus made great promises to the overcomer in the Book of Revelation, in similar fashion James elucidates the rewards of submitting one's will into the hands of the Lord.

> Come to Me, all who are weary and heavy-laden, and I will give you rest. Take My yoke upon you and learn from Me, for I am gentle and humble in heart, and YOU WILL FIND REST FOR YOUR SOULS. For My yoke is easy and My burden is light.
>
> —MATTHEW 11:28–30, NASB

The commands of the Lord are given to profit the believer. They are meant to lift the burdens off of his shoulders and to give him rest. Jesus lifts the taskmaster's (devil's) heavy hand off of the believer because He carried the sins of the world on the Cross and paid that debt in full. The yoke of the Lord is representative of His lordship and of the believer's submission to His Word. Only through total submission to the Lord can the believer realize true freedom: freedom from sin and its consequences.

The words of the Good Shepherd who has a gentle and humble heart speak to the world to come to Him and He will give them rest. Here again is God's great plan of love extending an invitation to fellowship with Him and live under His loving protection. As the Good Shepherd wisely leads His flock with a gentle nurturing spirit, so does the Lord lead His Church as they submit to His headship and authority.

"Lord, I'll do it your way," should be on the lips of the child of God when in the midst of the spiritual struggle of wills between God and man. When you can come to a higher place in Him then these words are said with joy rather than with grudging obedience. You will know the rest for your soul that Jesus promises the believer. Even in the midst of the struggle, the Holy Spirit will be with you to guide you and strengthen you.

Can you say, "Lord, I'll do it your way" as you enter into a higher place in Him?

CHAPTER 22

LORD, I COMMIT TO YOU

> But prove yourselves doers of the word, and not merely hearers who delude themselves. For if anyone is a hearer of the word and not a doer, he is like a man who looks at his natural face in a mirror; for once he has looked at himself and gone away, he has immediately forgotten what kind of person he was. But one who looks intently at the perfect Law, the Law of liberty, and abides by it, not having become a forgetful hearer but an effectual doer, this man will be blessed in what he does.
>
> —JAMES 1:22–25, NASB

An effectual doer of the Word of God is one who has truly committed to devote himself to the Lord with no reservations, holding nothing back. To achieve this goal, the believer must first admit that he needs the Lord and can do nothing without Him. Then he must submit to the authority of the Lord and give Him lordship in his life. Finally, he commits to following the Lord whenever He calls giving no thought to personal convenience or preferences. The application of these principles can be summed up in the term "working out your salvation."

The Apostle James exhorts the believer to be a doer of the Word. The believer must put some action to the Word as he feasts on it. Hearing the Word is the beginning of the process, however, if it is to be effective in his life, the believer must go beyond hearing to doing. If a person stops at hearing the Word only, it does not stay with him. It is as if he has looked into a mirror, but immediately forgets his image when he walks away. It is in the doing of the Word that the believer truly learns the ways of God. The effectual doer reaps the blessings of the Word as he applies it to his daily life.

> Let the word of Christ richly dwell within you, with all wisdom teaching and admonishing one another with psalms and hymns and spiritual songs, singing with thankfulness in your hearts to God. Whatever you do in word or deed, do all in the name of the Lord Jesus, giving thanks through Him to God the Father.
>
> —COLOSSIANS 3:16–17, NASB

The Word is to dwell in the believer's heart. It brings the believer wisdom, it teaches him and admonishes him how to live his life effectively for Christ. He is counseled to do all things as if he did them directly for the Lord. He is the agent of the Lord, his actions reflect on Him, and should be done in His name. Therefore, the believer's deeds should be the Lord's Word in action being done in an attitude of thanksgiving to the Father.

The Apostle Paul in his first letter to the Thessalonians instructs the believer on how he should live a committed Christian life.

> See that no one repays another with evil for evil, but always seek after that which is good for one another and for all people. Rejoice always; pray without ceasing; in everything give thanks; for this is God's will for you in Christ Jesus. Do not quench the Spirit; do not despise prophetic utterances. But examine everything

> carefully; hold fast to that which is good; abstain from every form of evil.
>
> —1 THESSALONIANS 5:15–22, NASB

Paul's instructions to the Colossians and to the Thessalonians reveal continuity and agreement. The believer is instructed to let the Word of God live in his heart and to do all things in the name of the Lord. How does he accomplish this objective? Do not take revenge. He should conduct himself well and do good things not just to other believers, but also to all people. Rejoice always and pray continually. Give thanks to the Lord; do not stifle the Spirit of God and respect prophesying. The believer is admonished to prove all things by holding them up to the standard of the Word of God. He should accept only what is in agreement with the Word and avoid all appearances of evil. The Lord does not expect the believer to meet the challenge of these words alone. The Holy Spirit's work is to guide the Christian in his daily walk through life to enable him to follow these instructions.

> Trust in the LORD, and do good; dwell in the land, and feed on His faithfulness. Delight yourself also in the LORD, and He shall give you the desires of your heart. Commit your way to the LORD, trust also in Him, and He shall bring it to pass.
>
> —PSALM 37:3–5, NKJV

Each of these statements of promise is preceded with a qualification. To trust and do good brings safety and blessings. Delighting in the Lord brings the fulfillment of the heart's desires. Committing your life to the Lord and trusting Him causes God to act on your behalf. This is how a Christian grows up and develops his personal relationship with the Lord.

The Lord gave my husband, Paul, a simple, but powerful image of how a believer is supposed to live his life. The Lord told Paul that we are not made to be like the Dead Sea, but we are made to be like the Jordan River. He explained that the Dead Sea is dead because it has no outlet. It just receives water, but has no outlet to be a source for any other body of water. The Jordan River is alive and can sustain life; it receives water and gives out from what it receives. Believers are to be conduits for God's blessings and power. As the living Word comes in and ministers to them personally, they are to share with others what they have received. The flow of the Spirit will continue, if we are willing to share it with others.

Believers are not only called to be blessed, but to be a blessing to others. The closer our walk with Jesus, the more we become like Him. Ephesians 5:1 exhorts, "Therefore be imitators of God, as beloved children." Our biggest hindrances to our love relationship with the Lord come from within our own hearts: our mind, will, and emotions. Through God's great plan of love He has enabled us to freely give our love to Him and He has given us great provisions and promises if we do.

He longs for your companionship and love. He waits at the door of your heart and calls your name softly to come to a higher place in Him. Can you answer Him?

"Lord, I commit myself to you."

CHAPTER 23

LOVE ONE ANOTHER: AN EXECUTIVE ORDER

> A new commandment I give to you, that you love one another, even as I have loved you, that you also love one another. By this all men will know that you are My disciples, if you have love for one another.
>
> —JOHN 13:34–35, NAS

Jesus issued this executive order to His disciples the night before He went to the Cross to restore mankind back to the Father. He called it a "new" commandment that would be the hallmark, or primary characteristic, of their association with Jesus to the rest of the world. Through the sacrifice of the Cross, Jesus reconciled man back to God and established the New Covenant of which He is the mediator.

The Apostle John recorded Jesus' earnest conversation with His disciples the night before His death in chapters thirteen through seventeen in his gospel. Jesus did not speak in chapter and verse; these designations were applied later to the Scriptures to facilitate their study. Jesus was concentrating on the most important things He wanted His disciples to remember. He knew their sorrow would be intense and they would feel abandoned, so He spoke the deep things of His heart to them to comfort them beforehand. But, everything He said to them was qualified by the "new" commandment He issued that night.

> The person who has My commands and keeps them is the one who [really] loves Me; and whoever [really] loves Me will be loved by My Father, and I [too] will love him and will show (reveal, manifest) Myself to him. [I will let Myself be clearly seen by him and make Myself real to him.]
>
> —JOHN 14:21, AMP

Jesus specifically tied obedience to His commands to the proof of a believer's love for Him. He began this conversation by issuing a new commandment to His followers and now He tied obedience to His Word as verification of their love for Him. Obedience to His commands was established as the only way to abide in His love. (See John 15:12.) Jesus promised to openly and clearly reveal Himself to the obedient ones who truly love Him.

Throughout John, chapter fourteen, Jesus pressed the point about love as an essential characteristic for His followers to manifest in their lives. His disciples had been trained and were now on the brink of walking in the fullness of the New Covenant, but they needed to be rooted and grounded in the love of God. "Now hope does not disappoint, because the love of God has been poured out in our hearts by the Holy Spirit who was given to us," (Rom. 5:5, NKJV). Jesus assured His disciples that He would provide a new teacher and comforter to enable them to follow His commands and to demonstrate their love for Him.

> But the Helper, the Holy Spirit, whom the Father will send in My name, He will teach you all things, and bring to your remembrance all that I said to you.
>
> —JOHN 14:26, NAS

All of the promises Jesus made during this conversation were all qualified by obedience to His Word, especially the "new" commandment He had just given to the disciples to love one another as He loved them. This was not a suggestion, it was a command issued by the Lord on the night before He went to the Cross. It was serious; so serious, in fact, that He repeated Himself over and over again.

> Jesus answered and said to him, "If anyone loves Me, he will keep My word; and My Father will love him, and We will come to him and make Our abode with him."
>
> —JOHN 14:23, NAS

> Just as the Father has loved Me, I have also loved you; abide in My love. If you keep My commandments, you will abide in My love; just as I have kept My Father's commandments and abide in His love....This is My commandment, that you love one another, just as I have loved you....This I command you, that you love one another.
>
> —JOHN 15:9–10,12,17, NAS

As Head of the Church, Jesus has never rescinded the executive order that His followers are to love each other as He loves us. Through the work of the Spirit, every believer has received the love of God into their hearts and the capability to love others as God loves them. The God kind of love does not depend on human feelings, but operates through faith. If a believer truly loves the Lord, then he can walk in love toward other believers. (See 1 John 4:20.) The love walk demands that the believer submit his feelings to the Lord's will. He must walk by faith in His Word and not by feelings of likes and dislikes, which can be easily swayed by emotions, circumstances, and the actions of others. Each believer is responsible before the Lord for how he treats other believers.

> Love is patient, love is kind and is not jealous; love does not brag and is not arrogant, does not act unbecomingly; it does not seek its own, is not provoked, does not take into account a wrong suffered, does not rejoice in unrighteousness, but rejoices with the truth; bears all things, believes all things, hopes all things, endures all things. Love never fails.
>
> —1 CORINTHIANS 13:4–8, NAS

Here is a vivid description of the God kind of love. If Jesus made walking in love the hallmark of His followers, then it must be attainable. "What then shall we say to these things? If God is for us, who is against us? He who did not spare His own Son, but delivered Him up for us all, how will He not also with Him freely give us all things?" (Rom. 8:31–32, NAS). "I can do all things through Him who strengthens me" (Philippians 4:13, NAS). With God on his side, the believer can do all things through the anointing of the Holy Spirit of God who dwells in him. The believer can walk in love—he is commanded to walk in love. However, it can only be achieved by submitting to the Spirit of God who dwells in him and allowing the Spirit's love to be manifested through him, thereby taking him to a higher place in Him.

Jesus, the Head of the Church, the one who offered Himself up on the Cross to reconcile man back to God, made this the hallmark by which the world will know His followers. Because He loved us first, we love Him. (See 1 John 4:19.) If we love Him, we will keep His commands as a true demonstration of our affection. There is no other way for Christians to live except that we love one another as He loves us.

Lord, help us to walk in love so that we can truly express our love and affection for You.

CONCLUSION

> Be diligent to present yourself approved to God, a worker who does not need to be ashamed, rightly dividing the word of truth.
>
> —2 TIMOTHY 2:15, NKJV

The child of God is admonished to show himself approved to God. His approval comes from submitting to the Word of God, however, he cannot submit to someone he does not know. That is why it is so important to develop a love relationship with the Lord. True love relationships require commitment from each of the parties to one another. Spending time together and fellowshipping is another essential ingredient for a relationship to grow and deepen.

The written Word of God reveals God's heart of love through His dealings with His covenant people. Jesus, the Word of God made flesh, is the personal face of God that the child of God can respond to in a love relationship. The Spirit of God, who indwells the believer, is the Comforter, Teacher, and Strengthener that enables the child of God to grow up spiritually. The believer has to be willing to do his part by opening up the door of his heart to the Lord and inviting Him in to be Lord. Once the Lord comes into his heart, He requires the believer's full cooperation and devotion so their fellowship will deepen into an intimate love relationship.

Full cooperation involves taking on the challenge of removing those things which hinder the growth and development of this love relationship with God. Changing priorities and putting the things of God first is important to every believer. Through the Holy Spirit's work, High Places of the heart can be identified and torn down enabling the believer to enjoy the fullness of his covenant with God. Walking in love, whether with believers or non-believers, will cause the child of God to produce spiritual fruit for the Kingdom of God.

> And a servant of the Lord must not quarrel but be gentle to all, able to teach, patient, in humility correcting those who are in opposition, if God perhaps will grant them repentance, so that they may know the truth, and that they may come to their senses and escape the snare of the devil, having been taken captive by him to do his will.
>
> —2 TIMOTHY 2:24–26, NKJV

Christians are called to be the Lord's agents and representatives in the world. As the Body of Christ, believers are directed by the Head of the Church to do the work of the Father: spreading the Gospels to a lost and hurting world. The Father's work has a two-fold purpose. The first goal is to restore more people to Him through the ministry of reconciliation.

> Therefore, if anyone is in Christ, he is a new creation; old things have passed away; behold, all things have become new. Now all things are of God, who has reconciled us to Himself through Jesus Christ, and has given us the ministry of reconciliation, that is, that God was in Christ reconciling the world to Himself, not

> imputing their trespasses to them, and has committed to us the word of reconciliation.
>
> —2 CORINTHIANS 5:17–19, NKJV

The second goal is that God's love may be perfected in His people.

> And we have come to know and have believed the love which God has for us. God is love, and the one who abides in love abides in God, and God abides in him. By this, love is perfected with us, that we may have confidence in the day of judgment; because as He is, so also are we in this world.
>
> —1 JOHN 4:16–17, NAS

The perfecting or maturing of the love of God in the believer gives the child of God confidence to face any situation, even the judgment seat of Christ. As our Good Father, the Lord God has invested all that He has into His children and has held nothing back. He contends for our love. He has made great promises to those who overcome the snares and hindrances that would choke their love relationship with Him. Those who follow His commands because they love Him will be perfected by this love as it changes them from glory to glory and takes them to a higher place in Him.

This is a process. He has patience with you, so have patience with yourself. Be quick to repent when you fall (and you will), and then get back up to start anew. He will honor your persistence.

The Great One who loves you is ready and willing to answer the cry of your heart, if you will open up the door of your heart to Him. In these days of uncertainty and woes, there is One who is able to give you comfort and peace. He wants to touch your life and let you know that He loves you dearly. Even as a natural father cradles a hurting child to his chest, so does the Father of Love seek to nurture and comfort those who will receive Him.

Listen, He is calling even now. If you will respond to His knock, you will not be disappointed. Take His hand and let Him guide you to a higher place in Him.

May the blessings of God overtake you and lift you up. Amen.

MEDITATION POINTS

- The Lord calls out with His offer of everlasting love to anyone who will listen to come to *A Higher Place in Him*. How will you respond?
- If you stumble, all you need to do is call out to Him; He is ready to pick you up and teach you how to avoid repeating the same mistake and show you *A Higher Place in Him*. Don't hesitate to call on Him.
- He is ready to answer the cry of your heart, if you are ready to let Him work through you, in you, and take you to *A Higher Place in Him*.
- He desires to hear from you and is ready to respond to your call.
- Receive His sweet words of love as He speaks into your life as you walk along the path to *A Higher Place in Him*.
- Spend time with Him and He will reveal Himself to you.
- He will open the eyes of your understanding on the issues that are important to you. He will help you as you press in to achieve *A Higher Place in Him*.
- Tell Him that you need Him. Ask Him to come in and fellowship. He is waiting to reveal to you *A Higher Place in Him*.
- Let His Word have preeminence in your life. Submit to His Lordship and He will reveal Himself to you and you will progress to *A Higher Place in Him*.
- Listen when He speaks to you and obey His instructions. He will show you the way to *A Higher Place in Him*.
- The Spirit is speaking to the Church today corporately and individually. Seek His counsel and He will show you the way you should go to arrive at *A Higher Place in Him*.
- Admit your dependence on Him and He will respond to you by taking you to *A Higher Place in Him*.
- Enjoy the advantages of your blood covenant with the Lord, which gives you access to *A Higher Place in Him*.

- Let the Holy Spirit enlighten you about His great love for you and His desire to take you to *A Higher Place in Him*. Let His Word be your measuring stick as you give yourself a spiritual heart checkup.
- The Lord is looking for you to give Him top priority in your life. This is the key to achieving *A Higher Place in Him*. Ask Him to come in and experience the joy that He brings.
- True success and prosperity can only come when you admit your total dependence on God and allow Him to draw you to *A Higher Place in Him*.
- In His presence He can reveal the deep things of His heart to you as you dwell in *A Higher Place in Him*. He can teach you how to live and be strong in the power of His might and to overcome every obstacle. He can bless you and enable you to be a blessing to others.
- The Holy Spirit's job is to facilitate the implementation of these things in your life. Let Him bring you closer to the Lord than ever before as you learn to live in *A Higher Place in Him*.
- Lord, I need you. Lord, I love you, because You first loved me.
- Can you say, "Lord, I'll do it your way" as you enter into *A Higher Place in Him*?
- "Lord, I commit myself to You."
- Lord, help me to walk in love so that I can truly express my love and affection for You.
- Listen, He is calling even now. If you will respond to His knock, you will not be disappointed. Take His hand and let Him guide you to *A Higher Place in Him*.

TO CONTACT THE AUTHOR

Mary B. Dovie
7530 West Sandy Cove Drive
New Orleans, LA 70128
www.mdovie.com